Love is the answer.
Denise Griffin

Testimonials for Hope for Humanity

"This is a timely and potent offering of soulful wisdom to encourage and support humanity at this powerful time. Full of information and opportunities for profound personal integration and interpretation, this book inspires us all to open fully as vessels and voices of Benevolence and Love walking and talking on planet Earth."

—Tayah Osâwâ Lanteigne, Vocal Sound Healer

"The book's title engaged me and filled me with so many possibilities! How can there be Hope for Humanity when there is disharmony in every aspect and event in our lives? Yet humanity is searching for the best possible solution as it is evolving and maturing.

This book is intriguing, engaging and informative in so many ways. Every page presents new paradigms and new processes of thought. If a person were to pick this book up and read a paragraph, they would have different levels of understanding each time! It is a book to digest, to interpret and integrate what you are grasping, as the words flow into a symphony of loving messages.

Awareness is the key to change, and this book offers abundant insights into the potential possibilities that we each can co-create in those changes that are calling to us.

As you develop the skill of awareness and apply the changes you wish, upon the experience, your view of the world must also change. By taking your words, actions and thoughts through the heart, you will become the vibration of the change that is Hope for Humanity!

This book is recommended for your new experience of Being Love!"

—Suzanne Steffensen

"The book, Hope for Humanity, like its authors, is a dedication to contributing to the highest good of Earth and all its inhabitants. Oh, the positive world changes the embracing of this information can bring! Its uniqueness is in the practical nature of explaining the significant changes in energy around us, and how to understand what is going on spiritually, politically, socially, and with our young people. It reminds us that our lives can be so much more if we work with the energy and divine resources offered to us, instead of going it alone. It dares us to believe that there is more to this life, and more after this life if we just open ourselves to the possibilities.

Are you ready to hear the message about the path to your potential? This book covers how to connect with Source, navigate the pain, release what is holding you back, and find your path to purpose, peace and joy.

Lessons – learning – insights – growth – understanding – forgiveness – transformation. We all have free will to choose in every given moment to co-create a life that truly makes us happy and fulfilled."

—Anne Summach

"Just opening this book made my spirit flutter. The title is so appropriate and something that we are all searching for in this chaotic world. Channelled information has been around for a long time. Some of us have been conditioned to be afraid of it. This book takes a beginner like me into a world that makes more sense and offers hope. These brave authors vulnerably share deep wisdom from their life and what they have been taught through channelled information. This book is filled with depth and the curious mind will want to soak it all in. "

—Cari Moffet, Author of It's All About Energy

HOPE FOR HUMANITY

LOVE is the answer...now,
what was the question?

Compiled by Bonnie Bogner

BIG MOOSE
PUBLISHING

*To my mother, Jean, for teaching me I could
accomplish anything I set my mind to.*

*To my clients and students, thank you for believing in me.
I would not be writing this now without you in my life.*

*And finally, to all of the beautiful souls who choose to live their lives
from a place of love. You are the ones we have been waiting for.*

TABLE OF CONTENTS

Acknowledgements xi

Foreword by Laurie Bogner xv

Symbol/Light Codes xix

INTRODUCTION: Why Hope for Humanity? xxi

CHAPTER 1 The Beauty and Complexity of You

    by Bonnie Bogner 1

CHAPTER 2 Change Unlimited

    by Denise Griffin 37

CHAPTER 3 Being Love

    by Patricia Meier... 61

CHAPTER 4 Love, Surrender, Trust, and Then Action

    by Ann and Bill... 97

CHAPTER 5 Return to Love Through Awareness and Faith

    by Anna Trillana 125

CHAPTER 6 Return to Oneness

    by Arianna Zimmer...155

CHAPTER 7 Humanity's Adjustment

    by Bonnie Bogner...181

CONCLUSION.. 206

ACKNOWLEDGMENTS

Helen Keller once said, *"Life is either a daring adventure or nothing at all..."* Why not pick the adventure? It sounds much more interesting!

I have a dream of touching lives and changing the world through the power of love. What better way to do that than to share messages of hope with all who wish to listen? And while I am at it, maybe encourage my beautiful friends to share their messages too, knowing the result will surely be greater than the sum of the parts.

This book has been a labour of passion and love, and an opportunity to walk through fear - fear of not getting it right, fear of not being good enough to put our words into print, and fear of showing up on a whole new level, for self and for others. What a worthwhile journey it has been and continues to be!

It is not always easy to sit down and channel a coherent message or to translate from spoken to written word in a way that makes sense. Sometimes the challenge is to know what to channel about. Other times it is to edit it into a concise and meaningful message, leaving some of what you wish to say for another day.

Dreaming, birthing and coordinating this book has been a great joy and a great challenge. Gathering a group of wise and connected channels, who are not necessarily authors, has been interesting, to say the least. I have loved watching each one walk through their barriers and produce a powerful message that is so needed in the world at this time.

Thank you to each of the authors for answering the call and showing up with their powerful messages. Congratulations to each one of you on a job well done. I believe we jointly have created something amazing. And one author in particular, Patricia Meier has gone far beyond the call of duty, jumping in to help all of us in more ways than I can count. Thank you Patricia.

I wish to thank my family for believing in me, supporting me, and putting up with all my crazy ideas. My parents, Clarence and Jean, my sisters Laurie and Deana, and my three sons Matt, Brennan and Kelly, I love you all so immensely and am forever grateful that each one of you are in my life. I could not do what I do without you.

My acknowledgements would not be complete without an extra mention of my sister Laurie who kept me sane through this process by being our proofreader and listening patiently to me as I figured out each step. And thank you to my dear friend Donalda, for all your solid transcriptions, unwavering support and belief in me and my message.

~ Bonnie

***

I have more appreciation than I can ever express in words to my friends and family for this experience called life. In that, I am beyond grateful for the opportunity to thank my husband, Darren Feser, for more unconditional love and support than I could have ever imagined was possible to have bestowed on anyone. I would not be here, doing what I love, without his encouragement, support, love, and care. And to my two most amazing daughters, Yoenne and Isis. They are my inspiration for change and a glimpse into a new future for us all. Thank you for Being.

~ Arianna

***

I would like to thank my husband, Jaret Meier, for believing in me and for helping with everything from encouragement to editing.

~ Patricia

***

To my love, Andrew, and brother, Ethan, you have both always been there to support and ground me back to Earth. I eternally love you both and am honoured to be in your lives.

I am blessed to be your romantic and business partner, Andrew - your unconditional love and patience has provided for us to live our dream helping others and the freedom for me to be as I am in spreading the word of Spirit.

Thank you to our students, clients, and friends who have been brave in allowing us to guide them to expose their shadows of fears and find their infinite strength within.

Thank you to everyone who has come together in this project, for showing up and committing to the contracts we've made together to come forward to unite as one to spread the love and truth.

~ Anna

∗∗∗

We thank Bonnie for having the courage to bring us all together and to each contributor for taking the courageous step in putting ourselves out into the world through love. Many of us have been hiding, not wanting to speak our truth, not believing that what we have to share is valuable to this world. Including us. We honour you and those that choose to read this book for having the courage to be you. Go team. Go team love.

~ Ann & Bill

∗∗∗

I wish to thank my family who has always supported my spiritual journey. This path has been long and at times painful, so it is with relief and gratitude that I share these channelled words with you now. And I wish to thank Bonnie Bogner for reappearing in my life, and for her vision and tenacity in coordinating this book. Finally, I wish to deeply thank the Galactic Council whose voice is both timely and timeless. This is their story.

~ Denise

∗∗∗

FOREWORD

When I was asked by my sister, Bonnie Bogner, to write a foreword for this incredible book, I had a range of emotions run through me. First, I was stunned – I mean who writes forewords except famous, previously published people? I am not published and I'm certainly not famous. Then, I was terrified – what could I possibly have to say on this topic? When I came back to reread the content after a break from proofing the chapters, I once again experienced the feelings of joy and optimism I felt while reading the powerful messages from the six contributors to this book. I then felt extremely honoured, as there are some incredible messages for anyone open to listening. So, "Thank you Bonnie; it will be my pleasure."

I would like to address the significance of the title of this book, Hope for Humanity. To do that, first please consider the kinds of messages we are inundated with when we read or listen to mainstream news. We hear stories of hatred and crimes against each other such as wars, robberies, and political upheaval. Constant ongoing exposure to these messages will lead us to experience feelings of sadness, hopelessness, and pessimism.

The messages in Hope for Humanity are the exact opposite of mainstream news. The messages in this book are filled with love and hopefulness. HOPE is defined as an optimistic state of mind, a feeling of expectation and desire for positive outcomes, either for ourself or for the world at large, and trust that it will happen.

So why is HOPE important to humanity? What advantage is there to be in a state of hopefulness and optimism, besides the obvious fact that we will feel happier? Neuroscientists have discovered that a feeling of hopefulness actually changes our brain. When people feel hopeful, the brain releases neurochemicals which mimic the effects of morphine. These chemicals can block pain and accelerate healing. The messages channelled by the collaborators in this book can literally change your brain.

Channelled? What does that mean? What is channelling and how is it done?

The individuals who contributed to this book are ordinary people with extraordinary messages from Spirit which they want to share with the world. They have learned how to put themselves in a meditative state, step aside, and allow the message of Spirit to come through. They have learned to completely surrender and trust as they open up to messages from others outside our three-dimensional human experience. As they surrender to the energy of Spirit, they are also in a state of peak awareness as they need to translate the messages coming through.

Here is a small sampling of some of the hopeful, loving

messages found in the following pages:

Denise: "There are so many beautiful pieces of love in the world that are not acknowledged... the Center (of the Universe) is in your Heart. You carry the love of all within you and it is the pure love of Source that is the key to All That Is. And you/we are all gifted with this. The challenge is to connect with it and be all of that."

Patricia: "What the world needs now is love, sweet love. All you need to do is love yourself. That begins with accepting yourself just as you are today, right here, right now."

Ann and Bill: "Keep surrendering to love and then take action. Love, is the uniform energy that is used to communicate whenever the people are brought together to make progress, increase vibration, increase health and to heal people. It is done through the vibration of love."

Anna: "If you return to love you know there is no need to do anything but to be. Be present to fill yourself with love by connecting and grounding within yourself and accessing your unlimited potential."

Arianna: "For it is all around you, wordless and nameless, for there are no words to give this at this time. Just open and receive the multitude upon multitude of gifts that are here to be bestowed on you. So beautiful, so loved, so Love."

Bonnie: "There is much beauty, and there is still pain and suffering, which is calling forth healing. We are here to help you learn to have this experience from a more peaceful place, that when accessed can allow peace, love and compassion to become your dominant force. Soon that light of love and compassion will bathe the entire planet; and, that will create peace on earth."

I assume since you have chosen to open this book, you have a desire to feel hopeful and optimistic. Through LOVE and HOPE, we can heal ourselves and the planet. So please, read the messages with an open mind and especially, an open heart. This is a gift you deserve to receive.

Laurie Bogner,
Hopeful & Happy

Symbol/Light Codes

During the creation of this book, the Galactic Council provided guidance that there would be one light code for each contributor to this book which would all come together to create a sacred symbol. The light codes were transmitted and drawn by Bonnie Bogner and converted to graphics by Jaret Meier.

There is a beautiful synergy that is being created that none of you can see the entirety of. Each one of the authors is a sacred piece to this puzzle. This symbol needs to contain an element or code for each person that is represented in this book. The resulting symbol will bring, in totality, the energies of so many non-physical beings who are speaking through the authors.

That symbol will be a crucial part of the energy that comes through this book. As each person sits with it and reads the words and thinks that they are absorbing information simply from the words, they are, in truth, receiving the healing codes that are placed within those words. When they touch or look upon the symbol, they are receiving the energy of the totality of the group that is bringing this information through. You may be interested to know that the group represented is vast.

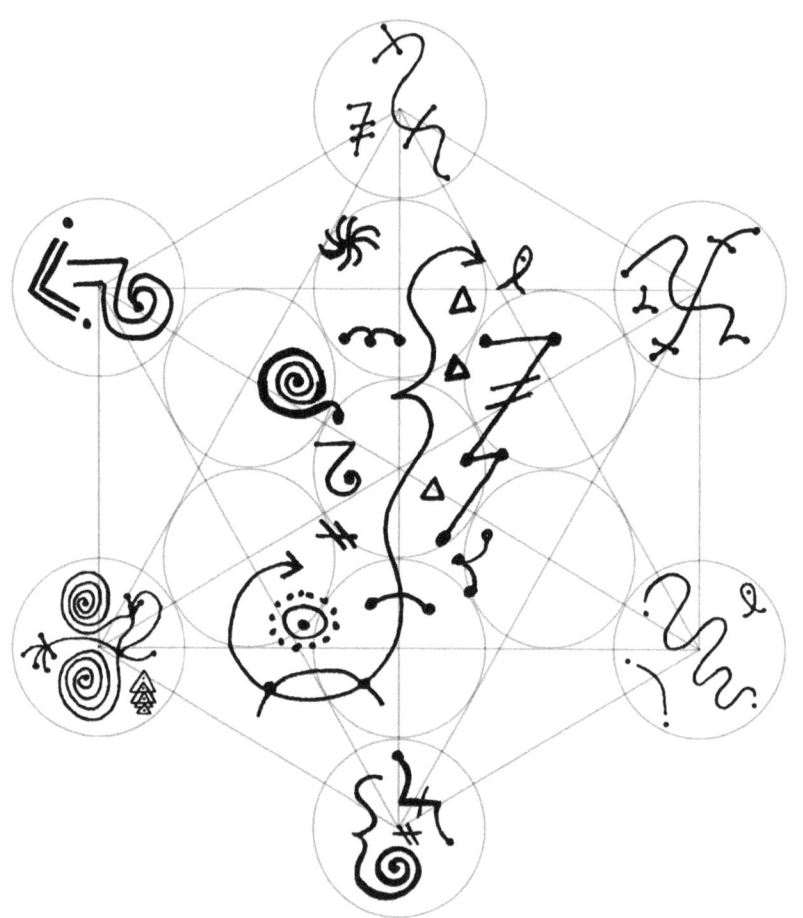

INTRODUCTION
Why Hope for Humanity?

Welcome and congratulations on finding a way to this book and the collection of wisdom it contains. It has been a joy for each one of us to bring this information into print. The information you will find here is varied, both in presentation and in content, yet the basis of each message is the same. You came here to learn and grow, but most of all to love.

...from Bonnie and the Galactic Council

You are at a time upon this planet when great awakening is being brought forth. For you to survive and go into that great awakening, you need to honour yourself. You need to honour those around you such as the plants, animals and the planet. In order to do so, you must better understand the energetics of this time. This is our invitation into that understanding of yourself and the planet.

At this juncture, there is so much that you are not able to see. And when we say you, we do not mean the authors, rather those that do not have the vision. There is so much that you cannot see that you need to know about in order to understand how much more there is. There is so much you don't understand and with that understanding, it becomes better. It becomes easier and opens the doorway to where it is that you need to go. We chose the title because we thought it would catch those that are needing hope and are ready to hear the message.

There are many who promote fear upon this planet. They speak loudly of it with the mistaken belief that they are somehow empowering themselves and creating something that will benefit them. These are the people who are sad, hurt and disappointed in their lives. They are trying to create something different for themselves by stepping upon those that react to the fear.

We are here to represent the exact opposite of that fear. We are here to lift-up those who are willing to be lifted, and to provide that ray of hope and guiding light to create a path that would take them forward into their potential. We are not just speaking of those who would create the fear, we are speaking of those who would consume it as well. Most who are ready and willing to consume, will indeed, consume hope more readily than they will consume fear when that option is offered. And when they begin to embrace hope, they begin to shift, change and come onto their own path, with empowerment and understanding. They no longer need to follow another's path; they are able to find their own. That is our desire for you, that you find hope and your own path forward.

Although we know there has been much rapid shifting upon the planet in the past years, there is so much more to come. There is a falling away, if you will, of the illusion of the fear that has been built and a replacement of that with the openness of love and peace, which is the true potential for humanity. This is a time of great growth which requires the support of hope. With hopelessness, you can do little, yet hope can do so much. So, all who have had that hope taken away and are searching for a way back to it, those are the souls that will be able to hear this message. Those are the ones that we are reaching out to. For in truth, you are the ones that will change this planet. It is not a few dedicated awakened souls that will change the planet; it is each one of you, and all you touch with your own awakening, that will truly change it. The authors of this book may be the spearhead, but not the entire spear. You are collectively creating the blueprint for that spear, for that new opening.

There is a beautiful synergy that is being created that none of you can see the entirety of. Each one of you is a sacred piece to this puzzle. This book will be bringing together in totality the energies of so many of us. Please understand we have been in communication in our dimensions as you have been in communication in yours, and we are indeed bringing this together as a group. We are, if you will, your ascension coaches and when we come together with you and bring forth that energy, it does not matter what we say or what you say, it is the intention and the love behind it that matters. The words are given for your human minds to have something to hold onto. The truth of this is the energy that is coming through it. As each person sits with it and reads the words and thinks that they are absorbing information simply from the words, they are, in truth, receiving the healing codes that are placed within those words. You may feel that you are a small group within humanity; however, we are a vast group that is supporting you in this. Never doubt the value that each one of you is creating by embarking upon this journey of hope.

...from Anna Trillana, Prime Creator aka Spirit aka Big Kahuna

"All you need is hope and strength - hope that it will get better, and strength to hold on until it does."

Hope fires the desire for an alternate and better path to unfold while strength to keep holding on is the resilience required until you choose to redirect your path. All the answers have been locked within you including the ability to change, the capacity to pay attention to the signs, and the understanding to interpret them. To unlock the truth requires the key of awareness, acceptance, and trust. This book offers you the keys to explore your soul and live your human experience with love, peace, and joy.

"To come back to unity, you must first be separated from it; to come back to love, you must first be engulfed in fear; to connect empathetically and learn compassion, you must first experience suffering.

To know thyself, you must first un-know yourself then proceed through the journey to reconnect back to your true self. To appreciate the stars at night, you need the darkness to allow them to shine through. To learn from your wounds and heal them, the wound must be exposed and triggered. You live in the enterprise of dichotomy - its structures define the Earthly dimension you are in.

Trust that everything is happening FOR you not TO you. Everything is orchestrated divinely in timing and in design for you to gain more awareness and learning, which are the keys to changing your perspective, in turn to changing your life to return to love. Your peace is found in the surrender to trust this and know that you are infinitely loved unconditionally, supported, and whole. You have all hoped for another way. You are always provided and taken care of. Here lies the truth you seek: when you are ready to receive it is given. You need only call and learn to listen and learn to see the love and light with you.

...from Arianna Zimmer

There is no formal grouping or name to the energies I channel. This may be because I am not interested in their being a name or group, or it may be that there is a far-ranging bandwidth of energy that comes to channel. This has not become clear. What I am aware of is that the energies are high vibrating, loving, supportive and here in service to us all. There is an incredible amount of energy that flows in for each channel and is there for each reader (and potentially listener) to access.

It has been a great pleasure and honour to ask these

questions and be a part of bringing the responses through for each person to experience. Much love and tremendous gratitude...In Joy!!!

...from Ann and Bill as part of Team Love

In your quantum space that you find yourself, there is a movement, a change coming. But it is not the movement of a few. It is a movement of the many. If you are reading, listening, participating in this exchange, you are already in the mode of considering and/or are in a state of movement. Oh yes, many say thinking about it brings about the reality. We say, yes, of course, that does help, but taking action amplifies it significantly and during the time you find yourself now, in approximately 37 more years there is a maximum amplification or possibility when you take action.

Look at your life. Go inside and do a little review. How many times have you found yourself wishing and thinking that things could be and should be different for you, but you don't take action? You merely sit and watch your life pass by. You don't believe, you see. You don't have hope that your small action could bring about the change for you.

So many in your world are unhappy in relationships, are unhappy in abundance, are unhappy with where they live, etc. We simply say, this book you see; one of the intentions is for you to understand that there is hope and then take action. It does not mean that you must end relationships or anything so dramatic, unless you choose. That is your choice, but remember, you make a difference. Without action, you do make some difference of course, but if you are willing to step into action, you multiply the effects hundreds and hundreds of times over. If you are willing to take action through love, then the world really does change for you. It changes inside first, then the inside begins to change the outside, and one person affects the next person, etc. The question becomes, "Are you worthy, as a child, to take a step towards home? Are you worthy to take a step by going out of the comfort of your own reality to move into the flow of building the dream of getting home, or creating a beauty?" It is your choice. These words are merely meant to remind you there is hope. There is hope for humanity, you see, and you, the reader, are the hope, if you choose…

…from Denise and the Galactic Council

"The Center of the Universe…is in your heart. You carry the love of all within you and it is the pure love of Source that is the key to All That Is. And you/we are all gifted with this. The challenge is to connect with it and be all of that. That basically, is the challenge of life. To find your Center, your Source, our Source, as we are all One."

We are all created with the same essence and our journey is to travel inside. This is the crux of it all. And it is the hope for us all. The Hope for Humanity.

...from Patricia Meier

Even where the spark of love in a hardened heart is just a whisper of what used to be, the innocent ones see and recognize. Feel and experience that whisper of love. They fan the flame with their smiles and giggles and goos and silly antics to grow the heart flame into love. This is the key.

CHAPTER 1

THE BEAUTY AND COMPLEXITY OF YOU

Compassion

by Bonnie Bogner
Wisdom of the Galactic Council

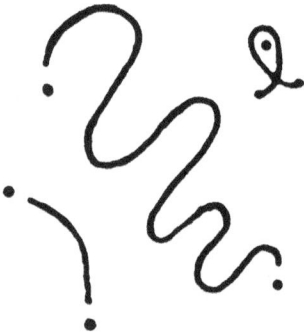

Remember your greatness as you embark upon this journey! Stay open and curious, trust yourself and in turn trust us. We are here to share our wisdom and to guide you, not to tell you what to do.

We, the Galactic Council, have made our presence known at this time to support humanity in the awakening they have been seeking. There are many hearts that are opening and awakening at this time. That creates a sense of compassion in us, for you could think of us as your parents or your grandparents. We are a collection of beings who have experienced ascension across the multidimensional and are now here to provide hope and guidance for your own journey. We have much love and honour for those who are awakening, for we understand the challenges that come with the transition you are calling forth.

It is a day for celebration when we see hearts lighting up. Do not even ask us if yours is one; you are here reading this book, aren't you?

Much of what we have to say to you is not new, rather it is a reminder or nudge to awaken your ancient wisdom from within. It is knowledge you all carry and have forgotten.

***

Greetings dear ones, we are the Council and it is with great joy that we step into your presence at this time. There is a grand experiment happening on this planet. Right here, right now. The whole purpose of the experiment is to further your souls, as you awaken from that deep sleep that has been pervasive for a very long time. It is no accident that this has been occurring. It is appropriate that it has been so, but now it is time to remember - to remember your greatness, your beauty, and your capacity. Most need help to remember, for they are caught in that paradox of right and wrong, love and fear, up and down, front and back, black and white, good and bad. It is a deceptively simple paradox and a deceptively effective one. In this paradox of contrasts, there is little room for anyone to be somewhere in between. You are either right or you are wrong according to the current rules upon your little blue marble.

Those duality rules are being upended now; more and more of them are being shattered with each passing year. As that occurs, there is a vast area between what has been right and wrong or what has been good and bad, and therein lies the truth. We are not talking about a definitive truth, for the truth is different for each one of you. And so, as it should be, there is not one truth, but rather a range of truths based upon perspective. Except for one, and that is the truth of LOVE!

The underlying truth is love; and, the joyful openhearted expression of humanity understanding that they are something more than they think they are. Their purpose is not to stand out or step above, but to be present with their brothers and their sisters, truly in their hearts and present to see the beauty in themselves and in others. For when you can look into the eyes of another and you can see them, not see the physical trappings, but see them, there is no room for anything except acceptance, love, forgiveness, and peace. That is the only capacity that you have when you truly see one another. That is where we wish for you to go, but most need a road map to get there. These words and these energies will help to create that map for those that are ready to embark upon the journey. Those that are not truly ready may simply enjoy reading this and learning a little more. Those that are ready will be forever changed, they will be incapable of looking into the eyes of another and not seeing them. It does not mean they will not occasionally fall away from this truth; it means that capacity once nurtured will always be present. Souls that have that capacity to truly see another do not go to war, do not step upon others in order to get ahead themselves and do not claim to have **the answer**, only **an answer**.

We see your capacity and we wish to draw you forward into that state of acceptance and love. We cannot do it through simply one channel or two or three. This needs to occur through several to create a set of fractals that become the whole. That is what each chapter of this book will be, a fractal of the whole. When that occurs, the light comes on in those beings that are ready, and those lights begin to dot the world so that those who are seeking find a way. Just as streetlights mark the way on city streets as you move from one pool of light to the next, you can see the next one ahead and it draws you forward. So too, the awakening of those who read with you and share in this information will become those lights that draw others forward and create a ripple; that ripple is what is called forth at this time. There are many names for it; it may be called good energy, awakening or ascension. It is about becoming authentic.

Humanity has so many layers of dogma- that is not the ideal word, but it is the best one that we can give at this time. There are so many layers of dogma that few are able to tap into their authenticity. Even to the extent there is a belief that there needs to be a war between spirit and ego. Why would you have been put upon this planet with an ego to simply stamp it out? Your ego provides a valuable counterbalance for you as a spirit. It is about learning to cohabitate, not to win the war. To learn to cohabitate, put the needs of the whole into perspective and understand that your needs can only truly be met if the needs of the whole are also met. You cannot win by being in competition; it is a spiritual impossibility. You can only truly win by being in cooperation. You can only find the way to move out of this self-imposed prison by joining hands and moving through the illusions together. That is what it is all about; that is the awakening; that is the ascension. It is finding the way to your heart and to the hearts of those around you. Know that you are truly all in this together and it is only through that, that humanity will find the way to peace.

We are here to support humanity in the ongoing unfolding that has been put into motion. We are not here to force it; we are here to encourage and support.

One of the things that has been happening in the past years that is different than it used to be is the ability with which you can change beliefs and shift what is happening at the subconscious level. It is becoming easier than it used to be. Just as it is now possible to wipe out or release and eliminate karmic patterns. That was not formerly an option. People would not have done this energy healing because it would not have shifted things for them the same as now. The vault that you know as the Akash has been opened as part of the ascension process on the planet. The Akash is opened to allow you to begin to shift and heal things more rapidly. The lifting off of karmic patterns, changing of beliefs, release of emotion stuck in the body are all far easier and moving more rapidly than they ever have in the past 10,000 years.

It is a beautiful time upon this planet, but it is also a time of limbo. It is a time where you are walking between these worlds. When you become fully ascended, fully awakened, and centered in your soul, you will be able to simply flick away these emotions. To say, "*Self, let's release what it is that is not working*" and self will say, "*Certainly, I will get on that.*" Just as now you may say, "*Self, I think we need to clean the house,*" and you pull out your cleaning tools and you clean your house, so too will the subconscious have the capacity to do that cleaning upon the direction of the conscious and the soul. While the conscious and the soul always had some degree of capability to give those messages, the subconscious had limited ability to respond. That was part of the lockdown that was happening while you are in a state of sleep. Humanity had things to learn from holding onto all of their karmic imprints. Now you have the opportunity to learn that it is okay, acceptable and even easy to let go of all of that.

That does not mean that you can simply do one single clean sweep through your body and release everything. If you could, you would only need one Transmission of Light DNA Activation™ and you would be awakened. However, this is a re-wiring of your entire physical being. That is what ascension is, and it must happen gradually, or it would overload your systems and burn them out. If we were to, all at once, provide you with every drop of the enlightenment that is truly you, and you were to release everything waiting to be released, you could not maintain your physicality through the transformation. That is too intense of an energy shift. While the body is strong and versatile and adaptable, it also needs an opportunity in the linear state to adjust to energetic changes such as this.

When your conscious or your soul directs you to make a shift at the subconscious level there is a bit of resistance from the subconscious because this is something new and different that it needs to explore. The subconscious believes that familiarity also means good for you; therefore, what is new may be a threat. That resistance is lessening in this time of awakening.

THE MANY ASPECTS OF SELF

Please imagine for a moment if you would, a massive and beautiful cloud billowing above you with wisps going in various directions. Going up and going out to the sides and going back and forward. That cloud is constantly shifting and moving and changing and the colours in it are changing slightly with each of these shifts. From that cloud, there is a narrow thread that comes down into your body and links into your heart and pineal. From there it expands into your entire being. That is your oversoul and soul connecting into all aspects of your entire human self. We wish for you to recognize and acknowledge that all components of self are crucial in order for you to experience alignment and harmony.

Now let us speak of the three selves: the conscious, the subconscious, and the soul. The underlying fundamental of the three selves is integral to so many things you experience in your lives. You are beautiful and complex beings and there are many, many layers and levels to your consciousness. We break it into various categories for the ease of understanding due to the inherent limitations of the three-dimensional world. There is nothing bad about that. It is simply different than the multi-dimensional; therefore, lists work well to understand in a linear experience.

Although we separate the aspects so we can talk about and understand them, there is only your essence and aspects of your essence. Some of those aspects are quantum, such as the subconscious and the soul, and some are linear such as the conscious. It is quite a beautiful structure and it is in place for a very good reason. You would have a very hard time operating in a linear world if you didn't have a linear aspect. It is important for the subconscious and the soul to be integral in what it is that you are doing, but it is also important to understand that you need that conscious aspect to get things done, to create that structure, and help to execute things in a way that fits in the third dimension. The conscious takes care of the logical thinking that is crucial for your experiences.

Please understand that the subconscious, the conscious and the soul all blend and overlap, and all are part of the same thing, but completely different with different functions. Each of those functions interacts beautifully and perfectly. There are, in truth, a million different aspects and pieces to that whole process, and while that may be fascinating, delving into all of them will not currently help you to navigate in this world.

There is much overlap or cross over from one aspect to another. Part of the way that they are able to communicate with each other is that they are completely blended at levels beyond the third dimension. It is a beautiful paradigm.

The conscious self likes to think that it is number one; that is the ego aspect that does that. We are not dismissing the ego. It is important. You could not have the experience of duality you are seeking without an ego. You could not learn to trust without the fear that the ego creates. Where the ego may cause a bit of problem for you is that it thinks it is the only one that matters. It causes the conscious to believe it is number one. The subconscious wants to support you in everything that you do but requires communication in order to effectively do so. If the conscious doesn't take the time to listen to the subconscious, you end up with a willpower battle which can be very uncomfortable. When they talk to each other, and each believes that the other is important, then they are able to be fully in communication with the soul. That is when you step into awakening and can be at peace. You are then able to see the strife in the world and bless it for all that it is teaching those that are experiencing it. You can see those with excess or those that have nothing and bless and honour them for all that they are learning and teaching from those experiences.

When the three selves are in cooperation, you will be able to more fully step into your purpose. It is not about naming your purpose, rather about living it. It is about being entangled with those all around you and honouring them.

The conscious and ego operate from linearity. The subconscious, soul and the oversoul all operate from quantum. That is one of the reasons that the subconscious must be the contact for the soul because they speak the same language. The soul has the level of understanding that the conscious does and the capacity that the subconscious does. The subconscious has vast capacity and the conscious has vast structure. It is crucial for those two to be together, to work in alignment with each other for that is the only way they can have seamless and efficient communication.

Now your soul, which is in connection with your oversoul carries your purpose. We know that we have spoken to you more than once about everyone's purpose upon the planet is to anchor the joy. The next step is that each of you has a different way of anchoring joy. That is your own individual purpose. Each one of you has a specific set of guidelines of what that is and how it is fulfilled which translates from the oversoul. It is something that you carry with you from lifetime to lifetime, which is one of the reasons you may find yourself doing similar things from one lifetime to the next. When you are following your purpose, you will start to remember and know that it is your truth. Please understand, you do not have to be working in any particular field for you to be following your purpose. You can be a janitor, top executive, stay-at-home mom, computer programmer or retail clerk. What you actually do for employment has nothing to do with what your purpose is. Rather how you move through the world and through your days is related to the purpose that your oversoul carries for you. The important thing about your job is that you enjoy it. There is far too much drudgery upon this planet at this time, which is not supportive of awakening. Expansion, opportunity, newness and enjoyment are far more supportive of living joy. You may still have some of those difficult experiences, for in their own way they contribute to ascension as well. If you become locked into drudgery and just getting through the day, that will shut down your connection to source.

Now please understand that when you have a non-physical experience, as in, you are in spirit form as the oversoul and having exclusively that experience; then there are not multiple selves. There is only the oversoul and all-that-you-are is absorbed into that. We will speak more about this a little later, but for now, just hold this awareness. When you come into this container that is called a physical body and you enter into an experience in something other than the multi-dimensional, in this case, living on a planet in the third dimension, there is a separating or a splitting of the aspects, because each one of them has a specific function.

In the third dimension, you have three primary levels of consciousness: the subconscious; the conscious, and the soul. Understanding the role of each one of those can indeed help you to function in this world. We will also speak to you of the oversoul and ego, to assist in further understanding of the complexity of the human condition.

The soul is multidimensional and operates completely from oneness. The subconscious is also multidimensional but does not operate from oneness, but rather from a place of protecting the physical vessel. The conscious self operates in a linear manner, completely in isolation from the other two, and has a concept of oneness, but does not really know what it is. When the three aspects can be in alignment and operate in cooperation with one another, you are better able to understand your role in the universe and the concept of oneness.

Subconscious & Conscious: The subconscious wants you to pay attention (go within) and may create pain to get your attention. If you are not paying attention to self, and something is requiring your attention or action, expect there to be some kind of pain, whether that is physical, mental, or emotional pain. Sometimes, it will actually damage the body to get your attention to save the body! We know that sounds like a conundrum of sorts and sometimes it is, but please remember, dear ones, that the subconscious operates in the quantum from a much larger perspective, so some of the experiences you have may not always seem logical and rational. And they may not be logical, but they are always with purpose. There is always Divine Purpose.

The subconscious keeps your body alive through functions such as breathing, beating your heart, and digesting food. These are things that you are not having to think about; therefore, they are the subconscious. Your conscious keeps your body alive through its valuable thought processes and by taking action upon impulses. For example, responding to the subconscious signal that you are hungry, the conscious thinks about options, such as available food, and then takes action to provide something to eat. The actions of the conscious are very valuable. As a matter of fact, they are as valuable to your existence upon the planet as those unconscious impulses we just mentioned. You may think those unconscious activities are the ones that are crucial for your life upon this planet. If your subconscious did not have a partnership with your conscious, the body would not survive for very long. The subconscious is there to serve and the conscious is there to take action.

Many times, your subconscious is the one that is in charge if you are not thinking through and being aware. It is very easy for the subconscious to be in charge and to cause you to do something that you may refer to as mindless. But just as it often takes over, it also requires direction. That is where the conscious comes in, for your conscious is able to do the logical thinking through things, figuring things out and putting a structure in place that the subconscious can follow. Without it, the subconscious would not have reason or purpose for performing its functions. Your conscious is what interacts with the third dimension and what is going on around you. Where the soul and subconscious may provide feedback about who and what is around you, the conscious will make the choices about your interactions.

The conscious is actually a very small part of your entire awareness, but also a very important part of that awareness. Remember that consciousness is your 'thinking being' when you are walking and talking and doing those kinds of things. It is the part of your self that makes choices, engages in activities and chooses new experiences. As you learn something new, you operate from conscious, and as soon as the memory becomes automatic, it has now moved to the subconscious. As you repeat something and you learn to do it automatically, it moves from the conscious to the subconscious.

It is actually quite easy to drop into the subconscious and become mindless. To simply move through life on automatic pilot, operating from habit and convenience, rather than conscious choice.

Choice is crucial in your ongoing experience in life and development as a soul. If you did not make conscious choices, you might never try anything uncomfortable or unknown. And you would certainly not take a chance and try something a second time if you failed at it the first time. The subconscious will look for ways to repeat what is known even if it is not beneficial. The conscious on the other hand, can make a choice to try something new, and encourage the subconscious to begin to learn new ways of being and to find out they are safe as well.

Ego: The conscious mind is sometimes misunderstood when associated with the ego. There may even be a drawing back or a recoiling from the ego, and in turn a belittling of the limitations of the conscious. We wish for you to know there is nothing about the conscious or ego to withdraw from. Each is a vital part of your experience. You cannot live on a planet of duality without having dual aspects. The extremes of that duality are the oversoul and the ego, and both are absolutely crucial for your experience of duality. Yes, you do have to have the experience of duality, that is why you are on this planet!

The ego is that part of the self that wishes to keep you safe by never taking a chance, telling you that you are not enough or that you cannot do enough. As the conscious carries out instructions from the subconscious and the soul, the ego steps in to say, "Are you sure?"

Ego is very closely related to the conscious. It is not truly the conscious, rather another aspect that can operate independently, but also synergistically, and in harmony with the conscious (most of the time).

Where the conscious is carrying out the instructions from the subconscious and soul, the ego is questioning if that is really wise, safe, and what you want. These two aspects work hand in hand, but they are not one and the same.

The ego is indeed a valuable part of your experience and ever so necessary in order for you to experience duality. You cannot experience good/bad, right/wrong, up/down, front/back, black/white without a duality opportunity and the ego plays that role opposite to the oversoul. It is quite perfect that they play together and against one another. While Spirit is continually drawing you forward, inviting change, and assuring your safety, the ego is questioning all of that. While the soul operates from a place of humble knowing, the ego prefers to boast and look for ways to acknowledge your importance. You see, if you only had the soul on your side, you would never even consider just how great you really are! The soul would know, but the other aspects would not process the truth of it.

This journey of ascension is not about punting the ego and getting rid of it; rather, it is about taming ego and learning from its challenges. The ego is indeed a magical piece of the machinery of this experience that assists in the growth and learning process.

Soul: Your soul (or higher self) is the overall container that connects to each your conscious and your subconscious. You see, all aspects are of extraordinary importance and you would not have life without all of them.

The crucial role of the soul is to be the neutral observer and facilitate connection between all aspects. It is not a direct linear relationship between aspects, rather there are many paths, and parts that actually comprise your experience of self. The soul could be considered the divine director to the physical experience, reporting to the oversoul and coordinating all other aspects.

Surrender and dropping into the subconscious (meditation) rather than staying in conscious control of circumstances is what allows you to move through from the subconscious to the soul creating a crucial connection between them. The conscious kind of stands alone in that scenario, where thought happens, analysis occurs, and linearity gets to take a seat. Those are all appropriate, but the close connection between the soul and subconscious can actually leave the conscious feeling a little left out, causing it to align with the ego and wishing to be in charge. This can create an experience of internal conflict, and we will speak soon about some ways to shift that experience.

Oversoul: Let us speak briefly of the oversoul. We ask that you imagine a little white, fluffy, beautiful cloud that is your oversoul and a silver thread that connects the drop of divinity (soul) within you to that oversoul. That drop of divinity then connects into the expansiveness of the subconscious and in turn allows the subconscious to connect to the structure of the conscious.

Each one of these clouds represents an individual within the Oneness. As those clouds move about and merge to become one big cloud, does that mean that you have lost your essence, your unique individuality? No, not at all, it means that your cloud, or your oversoul, and those other oversouls are in that moment entangled. There is a blending of awareness and exchange of information that happens amongst oversouls when they are merged. Each one of them still retains its unique and individual characteristics, but as they integrate, they support each other. Each one of those clouds could not exist without the existence of the other clouds.

Think of the sky being pure blue with no visible clouds. That is the oneness of all of us in complete integration (yes, the Galactic Council is included in this). That is Source! Then add those clouds or oversouls into the sky. Each one of you has an impact on reality, just as the clouds have an impact on the weather. As that little cloud scuttles through the sky and blocks the sun, it becomes cloudy, shaded or shadowy. As that little cloud continues to move along, the sun shines through again. Now, is sunshine without the shade a good thing or not? If it is a desperately hot day and everyone is feeling parched, that cloud and shade will be a welcome relief. If it is a chilly day and the lovely sunshine helps to warm things up, that cloud blocking the sun will not be so welcome. This little metaphor is to remind you that there is no good or bad. It is all relative to the situation, circumstances, your experiences and current needs. It is also a reminder that each one of you, even as that little individual cloud, can have an impact not just on you, but on all whose lives you touch.

We know that in this third-dimensional experience, there is much effort put into maintaining your individuality and keeping separate so that you know your identity and don't get lost in others. That is particularly challenging for those that have identified as an empath because your energy blends with others more than most. In truth, from your oversoul's perspective, this is not even a consideration. It knows who it is. It can merge and blend with all of the other oversouls and have no problem still knowing who it is, maintaining its unique identity within that merging. In the third dimension it may not seem logical to think that the essence of each being can be completely blended, yet still know who it is as an individual; however, this is not occurring in the third dimension, rather in the multidimensional.

In spite of the amazingness of your oversoul and the vastness of its awareness, particularly in this entangled state, the oversoul's evolution is dependent upon you having physical experiences. Whether it is here, in this particular experience, or other physical experiences beyond present comprehension, it is crucial for you to live lives, as that is how your soul grows and evolves, which in turn evolves the Oneness or Source.

We understand some of your experiences here have been

harsh and there is this hesitation to want to do it again. We assure you your soul is an enthusiastic one and it wants to keep playing, which is a beautiful thing. It may choose to play here on Earth, or it may play elsewhere. Either is appropriate, as long as it keeps playing.

There is much to this process of directing who is where, how they experience, when they leave and what they learn. It is a vast and complex multi-dimensional system that each one of you has input into. It is the merging of your oversouls that allows the process to unfold. **Each one of you directs your own aspect of this process based upon your responses, thoughts and actions.** The more that you can understand that you are a co-creator upon the planet, the more you can make positive choices for yourself.

Merging of Aspects: It is time now for the ego and the spirit to work together, to work cooperatively, for there to be an etheric handshake. This means it is, therefore, time for the conscious and the subconscious to form a unified team and work with the soul. The three selves are calling forth alignment, the desire to be in harmony and synchronization with each other. We know you understand what synchronization is; you are syncing your electronic devices all the time. Well, it is time for you to sync your aspects that reside in your physical being. It is time for them to come into alignment. You may ask how to do that, for they are so complex and at odds with one another. What we would say to you is that in truth, they are not at odds, each one of them wants what is best for you, the highest possible outcome. It is time for you to start communicating with each aspect of what it is that you desire. For when you consciously say to the other aspects of your being "I choose the highest outcome, and I surrender all that does not support that", all aspects of your being respond.

For example, your subconscious is having a temper tantrum because it didn't get fed the particular emotion that it is used to, maybe a constant diet of guilt. When it has that temper tantrum and it says "I want more guilt, because that is what I am used to", it is important for your conscious mind to remind the subconscious that the diet of guilt may no longer be for its highest good. Then ask the body and soul to assist in this process of harmony, peace, and centering in truth for your highest good. In that way, you begin to reconnect to the subconscious in a way that is supportive for all levels of your being.

Another example of this process is inviting your subconscious to begin to remind the conscious to stop and reflect on the choice to do something that is not in your best interest or that you agreed to because you think it is expected of you. These are the times to listen to your subconscious and your soul and notice what is really true for you. What would bring you joy rather than obligation?

This is a time of self-responsibility and self-awareness upon this planet – that is the stuff that awakening is made of!

Self and Others: Although you are all merged and entangled at the oversoul level, you are not creating for anyone else, you are simply here to play with them, not direct their play. From that perspective, it is not possible for you to control another and cause them to avoid their path; or for you to take on their pain to the extent that it will heal them. In truth, attempting to save another from their lessons will slow down their journey or inhibit their healing, due to the absence of their own experience or pain. Each one of you has come here with life circumstances to learn and grow, and while you can support and guide others, you cannot do the work for them. Your beautiful complex system and plan were designed for you, and theirs was designed for them.

Use this perspective and understanding when you reflect upon things you carry that truly belong to another. It is important to return to others what is truly theirs. You are not burdening them with their pain. You are giving them the gift of being able to process what they came to process.

EXERCISE TO CENTER IN YOUR TRUTH AND POWER

Please take a moment, dear ones
inhale deeply, exhale fully
be present with yourself

Invite all aspects to operate in harmony
for your highest good

Breathe

Offer for all aspects to pay attention
to each others' guidance
in their areas of expertise

Breathe

Surrender to your soul
the possibility that everything is perfect
even if you do not understand it all
releasing all the judgments
you hold against yourself

Breathe

Now offer all that does not truly belong to you
to return to sender with love
give yourself permission to learn
from your own path
and for others to learn from theirs

Breathe

Release that which no longer belongs to you
or which never did

Breathe

Continue to breathe into your center
and release until you feel at peace

Breathe

Your soul will be glad you did!

You can do this with thoughts, feelings, beliefs and
emotions, not just the ones you recently took on because
someone else was hurting, but the ones you have
accumulated from others throughout your lifetime.

METAPHORS AND MUSINGS TO SUPPORT YOUR EARTH EXPERIENCE

This is a collection of excerpts that the Galactic Council has shared over various channels. I felt that each one of these would support you in the understanding of self and your many aspects.

Commitment to Self and to Change: The human experience of time can be an interesting one. There is this belief in the third dimension that when I make a decision, or when I start to work on something, that it needs to be done and it needs to be done now.

You have all come in with contracts for lessons and there is an element of divine timing that is part of that. There is also an element of your clear decision to change things, to embrace things, or to let go of things that has an impact. Sometimes you simply must wait for divine timing. Sometimes you are working on something yet haven't truly made the decision to change it. There are many times that people work very hard on changing things without ever really making a commitment to the change.

The only way that you can know that you are done is that you are done! It is easy to say, "Well, I should be done by now" or "I wonder if I am done now." If these questions continue to show up, you are not done! That is okay, it may be that you were not fully committed; it may be that there were many layers; or it may be divine timing.

Just honour where you are at. Honour all of the progress that you have made and know that because you have done that work, you know how to do the work, and therefore, next steps will be easier. Honour yourself. Honour the work that you have done, and then ask divine timing to shift things a little, move them ahead or speed them up. It is okay to ask that you know.

Remember, although you are having a third-dimensional experience, you are a multidimensional being. You are not simply restricted to this space-time experience; however, if you do not understand this, it is very difficult to step out of it. Even those who have done this work for a very long time still get caught in the third-dimensional space-time experience. That is okay. Just honour yourself. Love yourself and appreciate yourself for the fact that you are having a human experience, for the fact that you are experiencing the third dimension, and in this moment, you cannot pop out of it into the multi-dimensional. That is okay. It is a journey, not a destination. This is not about getting somewhere and you have arrived. This is about finding ways to enjoy the trip.

Ride on the Slide: This is a good metaphor to describe the human experience. Think of your life as a trip down a slide at a playground. First, you are waiting to climb up the slide. This is your soul waiting to enter into a physical experience. While it is waiting in anticipation for its turn, it may be deciding what position to use for the slide down. Will this ride be frontwards or backwards, on the tummy or back? Will the slide be hot, cold, wet, sticky, or slippery? All of these decisions will affect the experience. And then there is the choice of how to react to the circumstances. Will it be fun, challenging, or upsetting? There are so many ways that the brief ride can be experienced!

The little soul gets to the top of the slide and that is birth.

They are born into the human experience and slide down the slide, in whatever manner chosen. Maybe the slide is hot, and the physical vessel gets burned. Maybe there is sand on the slide and it gets scraped. Or maybe it is a joyous ride down the slide and the little soul yells "wheeee" all the way. This is your life, and it has circumstances that you choose before you ever entered onto the slide, and responses to those choices as you are flying down.

When the little soul gets to the bottom to enter back into the non-physical, there are more choices to be made. Will there be a grand splash into the water, a thump on the ground, or a soft and gentle landing in the arms of others? But without fail, as the little soul crosses back into the non-physical, they are excited to have had the ride and are excited to be back home. No matter what it is that happened in that life, the little soul's response is "Wow, what a ride."

It does not say, "Well, I didn't get everything done, or I didn't buy enough stuff." It says, "Wow, what a ride. I think I want another ride on the slide." So, the little soul goes back to the other end of the slide, waits for its turn to climb the ladder again, and prepares for its next ride on the slide.

Now some of you, when you get to the top of the slide and realize what you have done, you wonder why, and you become determined that you will never, ever go down that slide again. That was an awful slide; you had an awful ride; you never want to experience that again. Yet soon you find yourself at the top of the slide once again. Such is the nature of the evolvement of spirit. That is how your soul evolves, by taking a ride on the slide, not by perfecting one single ride.

So, may we suggest you stop taking yourselves so seriously and enjoy the ride? Take a ride on the slide and allow it to be what it is. When you experience pain from the ride, do what you can to take care of yourself and eliminate the pain. When you experience joy, enjoy it, love it. Stop fighting for some imaginary destination other than peace, joy and love. Those are the destinations, yet they are not really destinations at all. Rather, they are elements of the rider.

Entanglement & Compassion: Entanglement, in case you are not familiar with it, is when you interact with someone else and then you stay linked or connected. This is one of the fascinating studies in your field of quantum physics. Many do not understand exactly how this happens because that connection is multidimensional, not third dimensional. While quantum physics plays in the multidimensional, there is still much attempting to reconcile it into your physical plane, which does not always work out.

When we speak here of entanglement, we are referring to the soul and oversoul level, not the conscious/subconscious level of carrying around the past or being drowned in other's emotions and opinions of you.

When you interact with someone you will have a connection or entanglement that remains after the interaction. There is a little bit of energy that connects your soul to the souls of others. This is part of what facilitates compassion upon the planet. Without entanglement amongst your souls, there would be no capacity for compassion. You would be completely individuated, and you would live fully and wholly in your own little world. You would not have romance, best friends, or the desire to interact with others if it were not for entanglement. The origin of entanglement occurs at the soul level, but profoundly affects all levels of your being and the physical experience.

So, as each of your souls becomes entangled with things that are a problem upon the planet, you amplify them. As your souls become entangled with all that is good and right upon the planet, you amplify them. We wish to suggest to you that you will benefit much from choosing peace, awakening, compassion and love to entangle with and amplify. Just makes a whole lot of sense, doesn't it?

Righteous Indignation: We believe that you have heard the expression that a war on anything amplifies that thing. The reason for that is because that thing is then getting attention, your energy and entanglement with it. There are many that believe that they need to be informed and stay up with the news so that they can be righteous and indignant about all that is wrong on the planet. We would like to suggest that righteousness and indignation amplify what it is that you do not want and invite you to let go of righteousness and indignation. It is time to see each being that you interact with as your equal and as your mirror. Even as you look into their eyes and look into their soul, you are coming to know another aspect of yourself. That does not suggest you need to keep inappropriate people in your life. If you need to move on, grow and shift, then let those people go with honour. Thank them for what you have learned from them, honouring them for the journey that they are on even as you move forward with your own. Understand that whatever level each person is at is a perfect level for them and their lessons; it is not a higher level or a lower level. It is where they are at and it is appropriate.

Your soul is constantly checking in and regulating your wellbeing to the best of its ability, depending upon your willingness to listen. It reminds you to focus on what is good and right in your world. Then as you fall back into learned habits of worry, your soul will remind you again. It is a cycle that you go through and it is okay that you are doing that. It is part of the learning. In this cycle of reminding you may feel a little out of alignment as you are focused upon fear and your soul is reminding you of love. If you wish to ease this cycle, we do recommend meditation, as it gives you a direct and uninterrupted connection to your soul and the reminder of what to hold your focus upon.

Spiritual Snobbery: We also wish to address spiritual snobbery in the world of those who are awakening, to their connection with their soul and oversoul. Spiritual snobbery is when you believe that awakening is somehow better than all other ways to experience soul growth; therefore, you are somehow superior due to your level of awareness and choice of path. While we honour you for what it is that you are doing, and it is our purpose to be here to assist you with this awakening process, we would encourage you to continually remind yourself that it is simply **a path**, it is not **the path**. And given that those who are on the other paths can also honour yours, then it can be mutual. The problem comes when someone on your path says, "I am better because I am on this path; therefore, you are lesser on your path." Regardless of others' attitudes or opinions about your chosen path, you do not fix their lack of honouring by refusing to honour them.

CONCLUSION

We have just gone through a process of breaking you into many aspects for the 'soul' purpose of putting all of those aspects back together into one complex, magnificent being that is YOU.

With all this understanding, it is time to simply BE love and learn to live your light impeccably. It is time to always do your best, and to do what you would wish to have done. Be kind, open and loving towards others and yourself. Look at others and know that they are perfect in their imperfection just as you are. Know that it does not matter what origin, height, weight, appearance, living conditions, belief system or career they have, each one of them contains a drop of divinity, just like you do. No bigger. No smaller. No better. No lesser. **EVERY body has a drop of divinity in it.** When you can think in those terms, it is much easier to be in a state of compassion to others and towards yourself.

Compassion is the underlying tenant of peace on earth! Know you must cultivate compassion with yourself to cultivate it with others. If you have a voice in your head that is constantly criticizing you, it is much easier for you to criticize others. You are one beautiful, glorious amazing I AM Presence. How does that I AM choose to show up on the planet?

It is time for you to be in alignment with your truth. To remind your subconscious and conscious that it is safe to be you, to be in alignment and to awaken. It is what you came here to do in this lifetime, to awaken - which requires presence, centeredness and surrender. It also requires the ego, and it requires Spirit. There is no one particular way that you need to do this.

May we suggest:

Meditate
Chant
Slow down
Be present
Stretch
Exercise
Sleep
Trust
Take time
Surrender
Open your heart
Be kind
Listen to your desires
Follow your heart
Breathe
LOVE!

It is a beautiful symphony that is being created by all these I AM Presences that are upon the planet and that are each singing their own song, yet singing it as part of a group harmony. Each one of you is singing the song of awakening. We honour those who choose to stay asleep just as we honour those that choose the song of awakening.

It is a beautiful unfolding, one where you will come to know the vastness of your innate power. The ability that you have to create that resonates in your heart. If you truly want to create quality-of-life experiences and connections with others, you must do it from a place of love and compassion that emanates from the heart. It is such a beautiful symphony and such a beautiful awakening that is occurring. If you could see it from where we do, we see these sparkles lighting up all over the planet. Where there used to be just a few sparks, now there are many, and more lighting up all the time.

It is indeed good to be on this planet at this time, is it not?

I am Ye'Yesh Ye'Yar of the Galactic Council and so it is...

Bonnie's Story

Bonnie Speaks: I cannot remember a time when I did not feel the pull to something more. I grew up observing others and wondered, "Is that really all there is?" Even in those early days, there was a deep faith that I could not articulate. Without knowing exactly what, I simply knew there was something much greater than what I was experiencing here in this dimension. But my friends had no interest in such things, and I had no words to speak of them; rather I would seek time in nature to be with that presence.

I was very fortunate to grow up surrounded by a loving family, access to nature and a connection to animals. Nature was my anchor and helped me to navigate a world I did not feel entirely at home in. As a young adult, I did my best to put this awareness aside, as it was not widely accepted. I even convinced myself that I must be making it all up!

Through the years I busied myself with running a household, raising my family and a demanding job. But this awareness was never far below the surface, and in the early nineties, the call to explore could no longer be denied. I began to immerse myself in the world of energy healing and metaphysics, studying, taking classes and reading at every available opportunity. This was a place where I felt at home.

The more I learned, the more I understood how little room there was for acceptance of this, in my very technical and analytical world. But a passion had been awakened and it was not about to leave me alone. That faith in 'more than meets the eye' was my constant companion and guided me through some very challenging times in my life.

There have been many incredible beings show-up to teach and support me, of both a physical and nonphysical nature. Some encounters are abrupt and course-altering, others are gentler and more supportive in nature. Definitely one of the most course-altering experiences was that of the Galactic Council making themselves known to me. I was not looking to become a channel; I was very comfortable with my Angelic team and the work I did with them. I had already created the Soul Alignment program (then called Angelic Awakening) and loved teaching others how to work with angels, intuition, and energy healing.

It seems the Galactic Council had something more in mind for me. They were patient but demanding teachers, constantly stretching me further and further out of my comfort zone. They lovingly taught me about surrender, stepping aside and allowing their voice to come through. Each time I get comfortable with one step of the journey, they provide the next one, guiding and lovingly pushing me along the way.

I know that I have not arrived at my destination, I am not so naïve to believe that this is it. Where I am right now is pretty great, so I expect where we are going will be too!

I love my relationship and work with the Galactic Council. It is my greatest joy to introduce others to the world of spirit, energy healing, and intuition. I delight in opening the way for others to learn to channel, or, should I say, as the spokesperson for the Galactic Council to do so.

Infinite Love & Gratitude,

Bonnie

The Galactic Council Speaks: Greetings dear ones, we are the Council and it is with great joy we step into your presence at this time...

Some of you may have heard that introduction from us before. It is our way of welcoming the meld, the blending of your energy with ours. While we speak through our partner, Bonnie, we direct the energy of our message to each one of you. We are a vast collective-of-beings that understand the awakening. For in our omnipresent connected state, we have access to all that has been experienced for all the worlds, as they embark upon an awakening experience. It is with much delight that we now support this experience on your Earth.

We speak through the oversoul of our partner who is known in her human form as Bonnie, and in ascended form as Ye'Yesh Ye'Yar.

We know that some of you look upon channel with suspicion or disbelief, and we understand. Would it help you to know, that each one of you is always channelling your personal connection to source, your oversoul and the multidimensional? Some of you are simply more aware of it than others.

So, who is speaking when our partner is coaching? Well, she is, of course, but so are we! Even when she is not in full-on channel, we make our advice known in whatever way is required. We are always working together and present in her sessions, because we know we are welcome there. It is truly a beautiful meld that we have created with her agreement. And at this time, we wish to express our appreciation for the opportunity to share this meld with our partner, and to have our words brought into the world in this book form.

If others channel our collective Galactic Council energy, you may notice some differences. This relates to the aspect of our group coming through, as well as the individual personality of the channel. We have a different relationship with each of our partners, so each experience will be unique.

I am Ye'Yesh Ye'Yar of the Galactic Council

And so it is...

What Bonnie & the Galactic Council Offer

We are truly a team, and while I (Bonnie) offer classes and coaching, I always feel the Council is close at hand, suggesting, guiding and supporting the process. Therefore, I make reference to WE rather than I.

There are several ways that you may choose to connect with our energy. Most of our offerings are online through the Soul Vibrations School of Light. We also offer distance and in-person personal coaching and healing sessions.

We also encourage Bonnie to take her friends and students on a variety of small-group sacred pilgrimages to places such as Hawaii and Ireland. When we decide we wish to take a group somewhere, we can be quite relentless!

We thoroughly enjoy connecting with all who are keen to learn more about what lies beyond your current reality and endeavour to create a broad base of learning so you may continue your explorations and connection to Source with comfort and confidence.

Website: www.bonniebogner.com or www.soulvibrations.ca
School of Light: www.soul-vibrations.thinkific.com
Facebook Page: www.facebook.com/SoulVibrations
Wisdom of the Galactic Council: www.facebook.com/groups/gcwisdom
Instagram: @soulvibes99

CHAPTER 2

CHANGE UNLIMITED

Gratitude

by Denise Griffin

with The Galactic Council

Greetings! This is the Galactic Council here to contribute to this book entitled, "Hope for Humanity". We are channelling this chapter through this Being as it was decided a long time ago that this was the process needed to reach many at this time on Earth.

We are here to offer insights and suggestions of various perspectives that may not be known, that may not be understood. This is the time for new ideas to come to light for the growth of all. We are so very pleased to be assisting with this transformation process for you all. It is indeed an honour.

Our role is to suggest. You can reflect on our words and see what resonates for you. We are all different. This is not like the merchandise "one size fits all". No, some things will feel right for you, some not. That is how it should be. So, let us begin.

The planet Earth is going through a time of metamorphosis. You have noticed animals in the news that are dying,

oceans that are polluted, trash being shipped to
third world countries, businesses suffering, housing
prices soaring, then falling, and food of all kinds being
questioned for nutritional value. Everything here is
changing – the environment, plant and animal life, and
yes, humans too, and their society. All is changing.

Life as you know it will be different in 50 years. There
will be many subtle changes and then some major shifts.
This will be as it is planned to be.

There are many forces at work to assist these changes in
the most loving way. Many are familiar with the concept
of Angels and Guides. These are the bulk of the kinds of
help that will be available for assistance should anyone
need to ask for it. There are many other spirit forms of
light available but the details of this are not as important
as the knowledge that you are not alone. You do not need
to traverse these waters of change alone. There are
helpers to guide you, in a canoe of sorts. They will help
paddle and steer you away from treacherous rapids and
always make sure your life jacket is on. There are many
stories of paddling your own canoe. We wish to tell you
that you are not alone. Far from it. We are here to guide
you and assist you.

The guidance of the guided. We are here for hope and
for humour at times, but mostly we want to provide
milestones of knowledge to assist you in these times
ahead. Times when you will shake your head and say
something like, "What is going on? This makes no sense.
I just don't understand why this is happening." We are
here to tell you there will be moments like this. Many.
And we want you to know that it is okay. It is change.

Change of all. Change for all.

There are many answers to the questions we are presenting. There are many who choose to answer and throw their hat in the ring of knowledge. We are but one of those hats and the reader, you, must decide which hat fits your head. Which one feels right and matches the direction you are going in. That is what we mean about one size does not fit all. We are all vibrating – resonating at different levels. As it should be. So, in this analogy, certain hats are more attractive according to where your head/heart is at.

There are many questions as well. We want to help make sense of some of these confusing issues that are around you all at this time.

Trump was sent to provide change. He is the stick that pokes the quiet embers in a fire and inflames it once again. That is what he is supposed to do. And he is very good at it. When change is occurring, there are many paths for access into that world of chaos. Trump is one such vehicle of change.

There are many challenges approaching for all who choose to notice. Challenges that will test your readiness for adventure and growth and depth. This is not a test to study for or worry about. There is no prep, as they say, to cram for better results. It simply is as it is. Those who hear, hear. Those who don't, don't. All will arrive at Source in the perfect time for them. We are all joined so it is a celebration of Each of us learning what we need to bring back to the hearth or heart of our Home which is Source.

This is how it is. This is how it was. This is how it will be.
We know because we have been involved and acting our
roles in all their splendour over time eternal.

And that is how things will unfold. A little at a time. It
will be an incremental change, piece by piece. Some
pieces are tiny, barely noticeable to the naked eye. Other
pieces will be very large indeed and horrific in nature as
that is as it is encoded. These are the kinds of changes
that pertain to the shifting of the tectonic plates in the
Earth that result in volcanoes, tsunamis and sink holes.
You see the Earth is changing too. It will not continue to
be polluted and defiled as it has been. Mother Earth is
changing too.

Animals are also changing. The whales are sending a
message to "Be Wary" - be aware of your choices. They
are showing Man the result of shifts. The whales are not
all going to make it through. Some whale groups will die
out and move to other dimensional arenas. Their work
here on Earth is nearing completion. But the whales have
much to teach us all. It is important to listen. They are
our friends.

There are many things to understand about the coming
changes. Knowledge is golden. Knowledge is eternal.
Knowledge evolves at levels of understanding for the
dimension of existence. This means Earth is ready
for new understanding. As we all evolve and grow, so
does everyone else. You may be familiar with the old
story adage of the 100th Monkey Syndrome. Once one
hundred monkeys in one area learn a new skill, then all
the monkeys everywhere have that skill. And so it is with
Humans and change; the more we understand, the more

we are.

There are many, many ways to begin to manufacture change in your body. There is the cellular level, the glandular level, the spiritual and the emotional, the mental and the physical. All are relevant. All contribute to the whole of your being-ness. However, all areas are needed to be engaged for change to move forward. This is because for change to be sustainable it must have a chemical kind of interaction in the body. We think it is our thoughts that guide us. But, in reality it is our cells that evolve and become something more. That is the process. It is easier for you to assume that it is the mind that dictates action, but we know it to be otherwise. This is a new level of awareness that promotes trust in the unfolding of each individual into who they are in each moment which is perfect unto itself.

We wish to talk about friends. Friends are a blessing for us all. However, it is important to know the objective of your friendships. Are you wasting time or building time? It is up to you. Some people are encoded to your hierarchy of best outcome. Some are superfluous and tie up your energy and are essentially time blockers for your future. You are all clever and involved in relationships with various people at various times. Use your heart lens to examine the objective of this/those connections.

This is not as simple as it seems. People are very shrewd about their needs. They are easily swayed by adoration or drama or fun times. Often at the cost of much more than monetary amounts. Have a careful review of your friendships. Have a careful reflection on your goals and desires. You will be surprised as you look through the eyes of your truth.

This is a time of infinite possibilities. Infinite change
and ultimately infinite challenge. There are many who
were not ready for this intensity here on Earth and
chose an easier path, an easier way, and those who are
here now are all courageous. They showed up for the
Battle of the Universe. They may not have theirs shields
visible or their swords drawn but rest assured, they
are in Battle attire. They are here to move the Battle
forward. To FINISH. It is a question of timing and back
up and surprise attacks and legions of support appearing
and multi-dimensional strategies beyond your wildest
dreams. That is the plan. That is the strategy and anyone
reading this is already in The Battle.

The Art of Change. That sounds odd as art is considered
something of design or fashion or concept. But we tell
you there is a design to the changes that are coming.
There is a fashionable way to endure or sustain oneself
in the sense of Oneness. There is a concept to remain
steadfast in your heart. We have all, as One Being, been
designing the Earth's transformation. It is quite an
intricate design involving layers upon layers upon layers
of history and lives.

There are Echoes of Change reverberating everywhere. In
the atmosphere that is increasingly dense with pollution,
in the Earth that is shifting tectonic plates and also in
Mankind's Heart. That too is shifting. It is important to
always be aware of your breath and your heart. They
really are the essence of All. They really are the most
basic part of who you are. You have a heartbeat that is
unique to you and you alone. Just like a thumb print is

used in police work for identity. It is the same with your breath and heartbeat. And this too is changing now. It is becoming more distinctive as some are choosing to remain shallow breathers and others are choosing to breathe through their heart. It is just another small part of the whole metamorphosis of Man. Subtle, is it not, a faint echo? Can you hear it in your heart? Stay tuned dear ones for more change.

So, there is an old saying that you may recall. It goes something like this. If you want to do something you need to be focused on it in your mind and then it can become action for you later as you do the action itself. This is because your mind is an important tool in the process of manifestation. You create what you say, what you think and what you plan. That is how it works. The Universe hears and acknowledges your decision of free will and provides that which you have requested. So, if you wish to change your "luck" or sharpen your aim or improve your life, do this.

Say it aloud.

Believe it.

Create it.

Do it

Learn to stop the self-sabotaging jargon messages in your thoughts; that is where the battle lies.

There are many issues to explore for those who are inquisitive about how this world works. In fact, it is an interesting process examining what learning there is here. Free will is the most discerning aspect of your arena of growth here on Earth as it is not such in other spheres. Each area of the Universe has specific learning and training and it is deemed so for all to "learn and shine in their own time". We realize that sounds like a cowboy song perhaps, but that is the design of Source: Love, Growth, Learning for All. That is the secret of everything in that one sentence. We are all here to love on multiple dimensions in multiple ways for multiple purposes and multiple lifetimes of growth. Yes, it is a complex issue to grasp but know that on our side of the Veil, all looks much simpler, much more simplistic in comparison to your world as we have the gift here of remembering. And that is the challenge for all of you to re-access your memories of knowing all that you already know. And then just Be. Yes, it is that simple.

There is much consternation about the state of consolation in the world. The world of politics is an amusing one from afar but not as amusing up close and personal when you are living with the consequences. We understand the process of learning to govern justly and carefully so that compassion radiates for all. We understand that there is a growing process of All that is needed to reach this place of caring. We also know that there are those who are keen to have the wealth and abundance here all for themselves. There is so much learning. This is a hot bed of political unrest and it is all designed to bring about change. Small at first in different parts of the globe which then triggers other areas and so on. This will tie in with a lot of Earth changes and adjustments, so it is going to be a bumpy ride for a while. But know that for change to occur the apple cart has to get upset a few times.

There is much consternation as well about the Planet's climate. We are going to address this now because the climate is the tipping point of the changes to come. Some of you are sensitive to this and feel the urgency that is needed to help redirect change as much as is possible in this time frame. These sensitive ones are programmed to assist, guide, teach, cajole and urge the public forward in climate work. We need more energy directed at this problem as it is growing as the population and pollution grows. This is a test for Mankind. Can the good of all survive or will the small percentage of those in power stay in control? It is really a political, economic, societal, and international problem of complexity that is difficult to comprehend at times even on our side of the Veil. But suffice it to say that Man is the Captain of his Ship or Planet and Man will ultimately decide as a whole which way the tide will fall. Man needs that momentum of love and change and caring for each other to help impact the factors involved in this problem. It is an interesting problem and not uncommon in the Universe for the population of a planet to decide by their collective energy what comes next. It is an agreement on a level of our consciousness that is beyond your comprehension at this point. These kinds of understandings will and can become clearer once Mankind reaches a specific level of vibration. What we can tell you is that the collective consciousness is not there yet. But it has the opportunity and the guidance to get there. The crux of this message about climate is this: **Honour Mother Earth, Honour Each Other**.

There is a lot of injustice in this world. Injustice on many layers of your society. It is structured that way. There is injustice in your judicial system, political system, government on all levels, education, media moguls, Google, print of any kind, Facebook...in fact you name the group and it is tainted. This is because these systems are fundamentally flawed for the elite to do well and all else to do so-so. Just as the Church has done over the eons. The structure needs to be realigned so that it resonates with the love of All That Is, of Source. This means justice for All. As All are One. The Three Musketeers had it really accurate when they said, "One for All and All for One!"

There is a decay occurring now in many systems. Injustices are coming to light that have been cloaked in darkness and deceit.

This is because there is an opportunity now for many, in fact all structures to reflect, grow, ponder and ultimately change or metamorph into something better. Something that suits all. Something based on love and equality and helping your brothers in spirit and physical form.

So, we are once again exploring the concept, the understanding of race. This is a word, a term used oft in your language. It is in reference to time, racing on the road, the race to get to where you are going in life, the rat race of society and of course the trump card of ethnicity and race. This is the one we wish to address now. It is about the inside of one's integrity. Your inner workings, your Soul, your Center is who you are, and this is not based on colour of skin, texture of hair, height of body frame or size of nose span. It is not based on physicality. This is something that is sadly mis-interpreted. You see, we are ALL different. Humanity is the same as elsewhere.

It is just the way the Universe is designed. We are who we are based on lessons needing to be learned. That is why we are in varying forms. It is the opportunity to grow and race to the next lesson. That was a little comedy on the word race for you all. You see we have humour but not all is humorous. The intolerance for your fellow man is an abhorrence that will change in the coming times. Accepting others as they are and as equals is the way of the structure of the evolving societies. This is a topic that will become more self-evident in the news as different countries struggle to accept these changes of society and the world around them. The world is going to become a place of tolerance, acceptance and caring. It will be a shining gem of Universal glory.

There are many times in the unfolding of a generation that enlightens the growth of the whole. By the whole we mean society as a group at that time. There are many reasons to assume that things are changing and that it is because of the political party here and the standard of politics in smaller venues or areas. It is all designed to be managed by those with the greatest lessons to learn, to teach. Some of these Souls are very evolved and are eager to assist in whatever way is helpful for them to advance the whole. It is a journey for us all. We are an amazing species, really - always wanting to grow and expand our knowledge and impact a larger area than ourselves. This is the code of the Enlightened Ones. To shine their light where it can be dark or grey or shadowy. Once a light is ignited, it **never** goes out. It may flicker, it may sputter but it will not die out. It is eternal. As is the light of Source.

Today is a time when everything occurs instantly.
Waiting is no longer kosher. You get an immediate cup
of coffee. You snap immediate pictures of what you are
doing. You drive your car to get everywhere faster than
you could walking or busing. You like things immediate,
not delayed. Think of dating today – swipe you're in;
swipe you're out. This whole instant society worship is
a diet for disaster. Life is about the unfolding of events
in the opportune timing. This is not always immediate.
Sometimes it is. Sometimes patience and learning
are required. This is the truth of time. It is what it is.
Lessons – learning – insights - growth - understanding -
forgiveness - transformation. This is what it is all about.
Artificial instant is for the movies. Organic instant is the
breath you take before the next one. Focus on that.

Every day is a new beginning. A new start. A chance
for a redo. Each day you are given an opportunity
to make this day, this time, what you choose it to be.
Better? The same? Not as good? It is always up to you.
Free will is everything here. Free will is the ticket into
this dimension and the one-way ticket out to better
opportunities for growth. It is an interesting concept.
You can do what you wish in whatever way you wish,
and it is so. There is no judgment from our side of
the Veil. We celebrate each step towards the light and
rejoice every time one of you makes a step closer to
All That Is. All That Is, quite simply, is Source. Source
is Love. Love is all. And yes, there are many, many
channelled songs, pieces of art or design about all of
this. We have been encouraging all of you. We love all
of you beyond measure. We are celebrating the light on
Earth that gets brighter every day.

So, each time you blink your eyes you are taking a snapshot, like a camera. And like your iPhone, the pictures are stored in your memory banks. But there is a difference in the kinds of pictures that are taken. Your eyes take pictures of your truth, your path, your journey. This is all of your free will. Again, we stress how you choose your journey. That is yours and yours alone to decide. No, we speak now of other aspects. Choices. The time of your journey here, the culture, the demographic class you are in, the support that you have. All this is your karmic choice, before you are even birthed into your new life. This is how it is. And you take pictures for your memory banks with your eyes and it is there to reflect on in trance, meditation, sleep, future lives, past lives, and so on. As you are a whole of many parts that fit together with no IKEA Assembly parts! No, your parts, segments join together seamlessly, silently shining, rejoicing and singing. There is so much love and so much happiness when your parts all come together. And we celebrate each step towards that with you. We support you. We guide you. We encourage you when we can, and we are here for you always. You are loved beyond measure.

There are many ways to unfold the changes of the coming rift. There are many ways to prepare for the coming changes in society.

There are many ways to build a better world. Let us just say now that there is no perfect answer. Many variables are in play. Many souls are evolving. The Light and the presence of Source Energy is growing. This changes everything. This changes the course of the world from chaos and darkness to Love. This is the way of the new world order - the plants, the soil, the insects, the birds, the animals, and of course for Humanity. The Earth is realigning itself in all its Glory to become a Beacon, yes, a Beacon of Light for the whole Universe. A lesson in free will results ultimately in Source, in Love, in Tranquility and the Unfoldment of All Is One. Because we are all connected. We are all One.

The impact of the Earth's metamorphosis is multi-facetted as the Earth is the foundation on and through which this planet exists. The Earth will be adjusting itself and reassigning parts to be put out to pasture, so to speak. And other parts will be revived and re-used to a new purpose. It is not appropriate for us to clarify these geographic changes as at this time it is more critical to get your attention. And to help open your eyes to change and new ways, new functions, new, new, and review. The heart needs to register the dynamics of vibrational adjustments to better equip those present to go with the flow. This is easy for us to say we know, but much more challenging to do when everything is discombobulated, and it is unclear what is transpiring. It is for these reasons, (and many more reasons that we won't discuss right now) that we want to discuss the importance of breathing. We encourage you to breathe softly through the nose and connect it to your heart through an imaginary cord. Yes, the connection of heart to breath is so basic, so primal and yet that is what we want to emphasize. Breathing, with cell phones turned, yes, turned off. Breathing with no TV, radio or media devices. Breathing quietly when you first awaken in the morning. Breathing quietly when you go to sleep at night. And breathing during the day when you take a coffee break or create a time out for yourself.

This is important as it strengthens the tie of heart to breath. And it builds a route for your heart energy to travel. It is good for this route to be familiar, comfortable and well-travelled. This connection will help to calm you and center your energy and prepare you to hear your heart. Yes, we said hear. Your heart is so very close to the word 'hear' - only one letter difference. It is not by accident. We suggest you practice listening to your heart and breathing. It will be a useful technique or tool for your tool belt. It will guide you to your Truth. The Truth that you have carried within since you were birthed here on Earth.

There are many challenges in being in physical form. When you die, you return to spirit form and you have your memory, knowledge and understanding of the Universe return to you. When you are in physical form here on Earth this memory is removed so that you can function in the Third Dimension. You could not reside here otherwise as it is too restrictive. Earth is a challenging place to be and we are very aware of the difficulties for you all. That is why we are so keen to support and guide your journeys.

There are many wondrous things about the Third Dimension. One is the need to eat for nourishment. We do not need to eat primitive life forms to sustain us. We are of Light Bodies and your food is too dense for our systems. We utilize forms of Light Energy. It is much different.

Another challenge in the Third Dimension is the artful manipulation of TV and media. You are what you watch, see, read and do. You do not know this but some of it is set up to entrap you into lower vibrations. The lower you vibrate as a Being, the easier it is to manipulate you as a worker, citizen or participant on this planet. The higher your vibrational level, the easier it is for you to resonate with Source and Love and the Brotherhood of All.

It always comes back to the same familiar refrain. We are All One and One is All. Or again as our friends the Three Musketeers said it, "All for One and One for All!

There are many items of necessity for survival. There are many items to hold you in place. There are many items to guide you forward. Let us explain.

Necessity is the items you require - food, shelter, and clothing if necessary. These items are basically for the body to sustain itself on this Planet.

Next are items for the good of the soul. They are for your heart and your mind and your spirit. This is your connection to nature and to All That Is. These are not controllable. Source is in charge of the higher levels of love and light.

Then there are items of restraint. These are mortgages, grass cuttings, car maintenance and the like. The things that society has declared are necessary for you to be here. There are variations of these restraining items listed that may be more applicable to your particular life, but we think you get the idea. Source does not dictate grass must be cut; society has according to your climate restrictions. Source does not say you need an expensive Mortgage, but society has encouraged people to have roots and build equity.

This is the time for opportunities and growth. This is the time to open your Soul up to more love. This is the time to see new choices. This is the time of all times. A time of change. A time of knowing and growing. The right hand does indeed know what the left hand is doing. The right hand is in fact shaking the left hand. All is coming together. But this is not always easy. No, it is a time of massive change. It will engross us all. So, what are these changes? There is a long list.

1. Society will change its infrastructure to include all genders, all colours of skin, and all races as One. They do this now in some places, but this will become a norm. Brotherhood of all. Caring for all.

2. The Earth will change its format. It will no longer be shaped as it is. It will have more water. Less land. More light. More equal sunlight. We know this sounds unusual. But bear with us – there are many changes coming.

3. The animal kingdom will change. Some species are moving on. Some are staying. Some new ones will appear. All as encoded.

4. The oceans, the water on Earth will be cleaned. This is a necessity. Dealing with garbage is a huge learning for Mankind and a necessary one.

The reasons behind many changes are twofold. One is the evolution of the individual Planet. Two is the evolution of the entire group or Universe. All affects all. This is why the changes here on Earth are so crucial. It impacts Mankind and it impacts then, in turn, all of us elsewhere as well. There is so much excitement about this as we are all evolving. In spirit form you are always evolving, learning, growing, transforming. And all life forms are doing the same. It is a wondrous thing to be so connected. We are really all from Source and really All Source and really all One.

There are so many beautiful pieces of love in the world that are not acknowledged. The items we discuss are not the branches of green touching a stream in the woods, nor the center of a rose glistening with dew. No, you are all familiar with Nature's joy and wonder. It is something deeper than that which we speak of now. It is the Center of the Universe. The Center is in your Heart. You carry the love of all within you and it is the pure love of Source that is the key to All that Is. And you/we are all gifted with this. The challenge is to connect with it and be all of that.

That is basically the challenge of life. To find your Center, your Source, our Source. As we are all One.

There are many ways to connect more deeply in your heart. Just ask this one who is recording our words now. This is a process to explore and find the method that works best for you as an individual.

We are watching those that are interested in this process and guide and encourage as best as we can. However, it is a process for each person of letting go, releasing and expanding, letting go and expanding. Like the breath.

It is a journey of years or moments, depending on your karmic path.

There are several ways to react to all the information we have shared here with you. Some will declare this book to be heretic and ignore the information. Some will decide the writer is not worthy or some such label. Some will deliberate on our words and dismiss them. And some will delve into our discussions of change and weigh what feels most compelling or what resonates loudest for them. It is a process of deciphering and deliberating on the paths you are drawn to. The paths of choice are laid out for you, but only you decide which path is yours.

The end of this chapter is fast approaching and we want to summarize key points for reflection.

1. There are no simple answers. There is a complexity of change coming that has not been witnessed previously on this Planet. Bigger than an ice age. Bigger than a tsunami. Bigger than a volcanic eruption. Much bigger.

2. Every living creature, plant, person will have a choice. To dance with the light, or not dance. This is as simple as it gets. If one chooses to sit out this dance that is fine. There will always be another time to dance. The light is always there. Waiting patiently.

3. The music for the dance plays on. In fact, the instruments are selected and the players. It hasn't started yet, but the dance and the music will play.

4. Play means so many things and yes, we all get to play and grow and learn and transform at our own rhythm. That is our own sacred dance and it is unique, and it is beautiful no matter how it is done.

There are many things for us to tell you about the changes and the adjustments that are coming. But we want to acknowledge those of you who are reading this material. Know that we will be with you, if you ask us, after you complete this reading, this chapter, this Book. Yes, we are here to assist you in finding your individual path to Source. You are unique, like a snowflake. No one else on Earth is exactly the same as you. We celebrate you - Your specialness and Your gifts. Because we love you and all that you are. Yes, we love and support and salute you on your journey. This Earth is a very challenging place to be right now so the fact that you are here says a lot about your Spirit's desire for adventure and to be in on the cutting edge of All That Is yet to be. We are so very pleased to see so many beings of Light on Earth at his time. It is a beautiful sight to see all the spots of light and love that are becoming so frequent on this Planet. And the goal of course is for all the light to join together so that All is One in the love of Light and Source.

The story behind the story behind the story. This is what this book is about. It is concentrating on next steps for us all, but it is telling the story of what is behind all the change that is underway. This is the part that makes it all come together in a logical and rational process. This is the way of change.

It is indeed an honour to communicate with those of you who read this. We have been watching you and awaiting opportunities to nudge you forward in your growth, your journey to "All That Is". We are committed to our work of change and transformation. It is hopeful work and we celebrate all steps forward with joy. We celebrate you. We honour your process, your choices, your journey. You are beautiful just as you are. Yes, beautiful. Your soul shines with all that you are. All that you can and will be. We love you. We celebrate you. We are with you.

And so it is.

The Galactic Council

DENISE'S STORY

It is a great honour to be channelling this message from the Galactic Council and to be a part of this group in "Hope for Humanity". Up until recently, I was a closet channeller who did not speak publicly about it. This project has helped me to step out of my comfort zone and step up to working on a larger scale.

The channel process begins for me with going into a meditative state. Once I hear a phrase repeated several times, I start to write the words down and before I am finished, I hear the next phrase and so on. This chapter was written in numerous instalments, usually about a paragraph or two per day.

After the handwritten work is done, I transpose it to the computer. I have been channelling for about 30 years. I see myself as a note taker. I simply take down the information and then pass it along. What I can say is that I love the joy of channelling and how wonderful the world feels to me when I am in that energy. I loved the experience of doing this chapter and was excited every morning when it was time to do another session. And I can also wholeheartedly say that channelling has taught me that we are indeed not alone.

My path has always been one of interest in people. Along the way I have studied numerous modalities of energy and spirituality. I worked in Social Work for my career. Now I am finding a new way with this book to assist and serve others.

I have two children and live in Regina, Saskatchewan.

If you would like to contact me, I can be reached at denisegriffin271@gmail.com.

Denise Griffin

CHAPTER 3

BEING LOVE

Connection

by Patricia Meier

Patricia's Story

There is a great love that exists within us, waiting for us to notice and return.

There have been three times in my life where I have felt the feeling of "being love". This is a feeling that is truly impossible to describe in words and, as hard as I try, I've found it nearly impossible to convey in words.

March 1991:
A drunk driver hit me just outside of my childhood home. Miraculously, I survived a ride on the hood of his car with a few minor injuries and one major; the loss of my ability to smell.

In my search to regain my sense of smell, I discovered Reiki and during a 2nd degree Reiki class I relived the accident and had my first experience with the feeling of "being love". This experience, as best I can describe it is as follows:

I fell into a deep trance and I found myself on the cold asphalt with sparse patches of snow on the grass to one side of me. The blinking lights of an ambulance were on the other side and I was on the ground.

I felt so alone in that moment, like there was no one else on Earth, so sad and utterly alone, more alone than I had ever felt in my life. Suddenly from above, two amber lights approached. They were amber eyes and I exclaimed "OH! There you are!" I floated up, following these eyes up, up, up into the ethers towards a bright, white light. Upon entry, I felt an all-encompassing feeling of love. Not being loved, not being in love...BEING LOVE. A blanket of adoration and acceptance filled my entire being with a sense of oneness and peace. I would have liked to stay there forever.

Coming back to consciousness, my innate wisdom told me that the amber eyes belonged to the Archangel Michael and it was he who had protected me in the accident and taken me to the light, if only for a short visit.

Although I would find myself connected to Archangel Michael energy in my meditations and Reiki practice, it would be many years before I would experience that feeling of "being love" again.

Fall 2013/Winter 2014:
I discovered the gift and beauty of sound healing. The two workshops spanned eight days and took me for one of the most intense journeys inward of my life where I used

sound in ways I had never dreamed of.

I was invited to do a sound blessing at Bonnie Bogner's for a reunion of her Essence of Angels students. The tones that arose as I opened myself were strange and unique. Later in the evening, Bonnie stated with confidence that I was channeling sound. In fact, she said, that was what the Galactic Council sounded like to her. She followed this up with a question that would haunt me; "Patty, do you know who you ARE?" I stuttered back, "Uh, I think so. Maybe…. I don't know?" She looked at me with a casual yet omniscient smile and said, "No, you don't. But you will."

It was in Bonnie's Soul Alignment II class, when I had my second experience with "being love".

"Step through the door," my partner instructed, "and look at your feet. Tell me what you see."

"I am wearing sandals", I said. They were golden in colour with laces that went up to my calves and a long, flowing, white gown. My fingers were long and white, and my hair was a sea of golden red cascading down my back in beautiful curls.

"Look around you", she said, "and tell me what you see?"

"OH!" I exclaimed. "There are children all around me and I am their teacher. It is my job to teach them to remember that THEY ARE LOVE and to not lose that knowing when they leave this place. I use sound and light to teach them to tread gently upon the Earth and leave no trace." I was filled with utter adoration for these beings who surrounded me and felt again that feeling of BEING LOVE.

Waking from this hypnotic remembrance did not immediately remove the feeling of BEING LOVE and I longed to retain it. My greatest wish is that I could bottle this feeling and give it freely to everyone on the planet.

Although I was unable to maintain that vibration of being love for any length of time, the impression stayed with me and any time I recount this story my energy rises up to a higher level of peace and calm. It is a key to the understanding of who I really am and truly, who we all are deep inside, locked up in our hearts and shadowed by our minds.

February 2018: I joined Bonnie and others on a Master Healers' Retreat in Kona on the Big Island of Hawaii. The following experience happened early on in the retreat.

Something awoke me at 1:30 AM, a sound or perhaps a feeling, I'm not sure. I look towards the window and saw something blinking. Reaching for my glasses, I was stunned to realize that the window is acting as a picture frame and within its bounds is the perfectly centered constellation of Orion. The blinking came from his belt. As I stared in sleepy wonder, I heard these words in my mind.

"Are you ready?"

I stammered back, "I think so. I'm not sure. I'm afraid." At which point I fell back into a deep sleep.

The next night I was again awoken by the lights and before the question was even asked, I stated, "Yes! Yes! I am ready!" I felt the top of my head tingle and heat up as if someone were pouring warm honey over it. My body vibrated in a beautiful and pleasing way, where upon I feel back into a deep sleep. In the morning, when I awoke, I had the third blessed experience of BEING LOVE. I basked in the vibration until it faded, and I became grounded enough to be able to wander my way downstairs to share my experience.

I firmly believe that this feeling is available to all of us when we choose it. We are all LOVE at our core. We are all Sparks of One Divine Light - a Unified Field of Existence - and we are here with a prime directive of experiencing the polarities of a human life. We are here to know the light and the dark, the good and the bad, the right and the wrong, as well as the masculine and feminine polarities here on Earth.

All choices, all ideas in creation and all experiences exist for us. We have the gift of Free Will and can choose to act on any ideas which arise. Our goal is to return to LOVE, to return to the unified field where we are all one, vibrating as LOVE and LIGHT. The spark that lives in our heart and pulses with our breath knows this to be true.

My Hope for Humanity is that we all find the love within us, that we all shine the light from our heart as brightly as those students in my school of One Heart One Voice. This love is enough to light the way for humanity to not just exist but to thrive in a world where everyone has enough; where everyone lives a life of passion and joyful pursuits. I believe it is possible. I believe we can get there and that finding a harmonic balance is our grand collaborative goal. These times we live in are the most challenging because they hold the greatest reward. Our victory in choosing a life of love will resound throughout the universe and correct, clean, and balance everything in existence.

My chapter captures the questions I have asked my team, who I refer to as The Light of Orion, along with the Galactic Council; my own insights are included at the end of each question where required.

Personally, I will continuc to shine my light and share my stories with anyone who asks. My hope is that my light can be a Spark of Healing to ignite the next and the next and the next person until we all shine as bright as Orion in the Hawaiian sky.

Much love,

Patricia Meier

www.sparksofhealing.ca
patricia.meier@sparksofhealing.ca
www.facebook.com/sparksofhealing
www.instagram.com/sparksofhealing
www.linkedin.com/in/sparksofhealing

WHAT IS THE PURPOSE OF THE GENERAL UNREST IN THE WORLD AT THIS TIME?

(I.E. LABOUR, POLITICAL, ENVIRONMENTAL, RACIAL & GENDER)

Oh, dear one. There is so much going on planet Earth right now. There are many who see that they are no longer happy or satisfied with the status quo of the Earth's rules and structures.

The children did not come here to play along with the way things are. They came here to make a difference. These children are gentle souls with youthful energy and carefree attitudes. Don't kid yourself; they do care, very much. They simply do not care to, nor have time to wait until they are older to be seen and heard.

These kids know that they must act now, so they "act up" to be noticed. They will lead the way to the changes that are necessary. They are not interested in hearing why their ideas will not work as they are far too busy getting them done. They will lead the way. They are following their hearts, their love of the Earth, and all the wonderful creations that live here with us.

The old ways must crack and crumble. People are tired of being pushed down again and again, like children told to wait their turn, put in their time, and wait until they are older to have control over their lives. They don't wish to wait. There is an urgency in the hearts of those who are beginning to awaken. Some cannot say why they feel the way they do, only that they know they must do something, and it must be now. The people are banding together. They are talking in ways that allow them to be open and honest without the worry of those around them overhearing. They are using the technology to find kindred minds and hearts. They are finding that their feelings are valid and that they are not alone.

In a lot of cases it is getting harder for people to be held down by "the man". People are tasting of freedom of thought and wanting the freedom of action.

The youth in corporate worlds are not staying forever. They recognize where they do not fit and leave for more suitable options. Others, who have been in these places for large portions of their lives stand by with jaws agape. They do not understand the audacity, as they see it, of the young people walking away from "good jobs". It is because the youth have awakened and are following their hearts. They know what they want and what they don't want. They slip the chains that bind those who have been imprisoned by old belief systems.

They are demanding a new way - a way that honours all as equal and a way where no one goes hungry or cold. There are many from all walks of life who are beginning to demand these changes.

Humanity is on the precipice of a huge leap forward. This is the center, the mid way, the turning point. People are feeling left behind and exhausted in doing the day to day. People are seeking a change. The old regime will not let go of the reins easily, but it is time. There must be a desire to, instead of taking over the reins, let the horses run free to explore and enjoy this world we live in.

A return to somewhat simpler times where the hoarding stops. Where people instead, collect the love from one another's hearts and measure the value of their lives by the number of friends they hold tight. A life where value is measured by the number of hugs traded in a day and the richness of looking deeply into another human's eyes. By connecting to the meaning and depth of another's message, we feel their hearts and move forward together in a united goal where everyone wins.

The people are changing, and the new generations are no longer content to just tow the line and walk in the worn paths of those before. They wish to forge new roadways where the scenery is crisp and clean, where they are the masters of their own destiny without sacrificing the harmony and beauty of the planet.

You ask what the purpose is? The purpose is that it is time for a change, a shift in priority, and an inclusion of all peoples in health, harmony, and love.

It is time. It is coming and it is grand in its design. Have no fear of these changes although they may be uncomfortable. They are necessary and the vision of the other side of this change is worth the perspiration of the effort. Love is the answer. Love yourself and those around you even during the difficult days of this shift. It is all worth the effort. We promise. Go forward with your heart in the lead and see what treasures you may uncover on the journey ahead.

Patricia's insights: In this context, "the children" refers to those in the 18–30 age range. Originally, this question was about labour disputes, but the answer given covers so much more than that. For this reason, I have changed the question to encompass all that they had to say.

WHY ARE WE LOSING SO MANY OF TODAY'S YOUTH TO SUICIDE AND DRUG OVERDOSES? WHAT ARE EXIT POINTS?

I have asked this question of the Galactic Council.

Oh, dear one, we know you feel the pain of the loss of so many. Please understand that there are exit points that each person in life can choose to partake in. There is a joy in leaving just as there is joy in entering the earth's plane. We know this is hard for you to comprehend. Please understand that we all come here with work to do and contracts to fulfill. When we are done, when it is complete, we may choose to leave this earth plane. We watch from the other side for a while to see the full outcome of our acts. We may choose to come again to take on different tasks in different places in different bodies in different situations. It is all choice. It is all free will.

The youth of today have come here with open hearts to help the earth and its people to change the course of humanity for a better choice, a higher mind choice, and it is hard for them to be here.

Do you know that you assist them with the message that they make a difference just by being here? The message that their presence is enough? As they bring the loving-kindness energy with them from their birth, they plant that loving-kindness in the soul of our Mother Gaia when they step down upon her. They are planting seeds of love which will blossom and grow. It is magical and immediate. (I am presented with a picture of a child running and everywhere their little feet touch down; grass and tiny flowers spring up magically.)

It is all right if they do not stay for long. Yes, their parents weep. May their tears wipe away the motes from their eyes so they can see what truly matters at this time on this earth. The loss will shake them out of their complacency of accepting what is without thought, and instead will move them to choose a life with intention and attention, a life that is lived with purpose and determination of creating a better world for all.

A loss of a child is the ultimate shake up. Yes, some of these children have come here with the intention to leave early. People in third world countries lose their children daily to poverty and sickness. The only way for the first world countries to experience the volume of loss is through an act which appears to be an intention to leave. The way to shake the Americas out of their complacency is to have their masses experience loss of loved ones.

You are thinking this is harsh and this message is not one to share. Yet, you asked the question. Do not judge the message right or wrong. You know in your heart that your trajectory changed upon losing your daughter from one of corporate greed and climbing to one of basic need for love and understanding. You would not be seeking the lessons and being of non-judgment had this not occurred in your life. You have said as much yourself. The world needs change fast and hard and now. Loss brings out love and loving acts of support. It brings a realization from deep inside the heart of what is truly important, what truly matters in this life experience. It is the ultimate shake up to lose a child. These children's souls have come here with the purpose of shaking up the world out of its fitful sleep, and to open the eyes of the world for a need to change our focus. That is all.

Patricia's insights: Exit points are times where the soul may choose to stop living the current life. In my own experience, after a serious car accident, my perception of death and life changed dramatically. I went on to live a challenging life with deep and meaningful experiences for myself and to share with others. I believe I could have left then, but chose to continue.

I did lose my only daughter to a brain tumour in 2007 when she was five years old. The diagnosis shifted my priorities in life completely around and softened me back to who I truly was at heart. I let go of running full bore trying to become one of the boys and returned to my feminine aspect of nurturing, loving, and learning to be cared for by others. The lessons I learned from this experience made me a better person and inspired me to change the trajectory of my life path.

WHAT ARE THE LESSONS OF MONEY?

More money never ever equates with more happiness. True wealth is in the way we spend our energy, not the size of our bank accounts.

Money is a poor substitute for the exchange of energy. Money was intended as an IOU for times when the receiver did not have anything that the giver needed immediately. The best cultures knew that all persons had their worth and that all exchanges would balance in time.

At this time, some people are more concerned with fair share than with considering all types of work as worthwhile and equal. One man will have no food, while another man has spoilage. Humanity is at a point where we are waking up to feel the pain and suffering of our brothers and sisters and understanding that their pain is ours, and ours is theirs. Opening our hearts to feel the feelings of the world and all the things that reside within it. It is no accident that the world's changes are happening at a time where the news travels at light speeds, where one person can easily find that they are not alone in their suffering or in their opinion that things are not right.

The internet is a gift from the gods, not a gift from the nerds. It was intended as a tool to bring you together and not an end in itself. The world wide web was meant as a steppingstone to the true divine web of interconnected hearts, minds, and souls. It is like a child's rendering of the Eiffel Tower in Lego blocks. Please understand, dear ones, that it is time to wake up and create that web of light and love. It is time to connect with one another like the world, the Earth, has never seen, felt, or experienced before. Come together my beloveds and feel the power of hearts conjoined.

Together you can change and shift the light to create a world so worth saving. The Earth was a gift to the experiencers by the creators. Yet we are all creators who cannot see the entirety of the gift we have been given. Please open your eyes and see the beauty around you. Love the Earth and all her wonders.

Patricia's insights: Sharing of the information at light speed has its own polarity. Information sharing can have a positive impact and it can also have a negative impact on the world. The key here is that each of us have Free Will to choose what to believe and how to act in response to the information we are taking in. As with anything there are two sides to the coin. The key here is to act in a way that demonstrates loving kindness.

It is interesting to consider that the internet is a mechanical way for people to have instant transference of their inner thoughts and feelings. I wonder if this is an attempt to return to a time where telepathy was the norm for a previous incarnation of humanity?

WHY ARE YOUNG PEOPLE TAKING SUCH A LEADERSHIP ROLE AT THIS TIME?

Whitney Houston had the right idea years ago when she sang, "I believe that children are our future. Teach them well and let them lead the way."

With increasing numbers, children today refuse to identify themselves as male or female and preferring to be non-binary. This presents a problem for large parts of society and why is that? Why do people in power especially, care so much about how someone else chooses to identify themselves? It is because it upsets the order that has been so carefully constructed over time by the rule makers.

Right now, our Earth is very much driven by a masculine versus the feminine aspect of energy. Before going further, it would be helpful to define feminine and masculine polarity. Feminine and masculine, for the purposes of this exploration, does not refer to the same set of societal differences as male and female. Male and female at its core is based on which body parts we possess for procreation along with a cornucopia of rules and regulations that society has wrapped around those distinctions. These rules and regulations hold both genders hostage within doctrines that really and truly do not make sense in today's day and age. Masculine and feminine for this purpose refers to the approaches inherent within those energies and the polarities they possess in a complimentary fashion.

The masculine energy is associated with colonization, order, and structure. Exploration, claiming, and conquering have been the way of much of the recorded history of the human legacy that we live in today. A big part of that structure is the need to categorize everything. Labelling things or people puts them in a box, creating expectations of them based on predefined labels. Everything has a definition; a predetermined understanding and all the knowns are known to those around them.

In this set of societal rules, boys wear blue and are expected to be the breadwinner, to be the protector in roles like policeman, fireman, doctor, lawyer and the armed forces. Girls wear pink and are the homemakers, waitresses, nurses, and stewardesses. This is more on the caretaking spectrum and less of the decision maker for society overall.

The children of today are turning into the youth of today, the inventors, the thinkers and the voters of tomorrow. Many of these children refuse to get into the predefined boxes and heaven help anyone who forces them into a box. They will rip, tear and burn that box for their freedom. They question rather than accept what is written in the rulebook viewing everything as malleable and open to improvement.

How wonderful that these children are in touch with both aspects of humanity's polarity. Maybe having a more balanced perspective will help them see our planet as more than just a commodity to be bought and sold.

If we hold to the premise that we are all part of one original source who have come as spiritual beings having a human existence, then we can agree that we have come from a unified source of love and light to experience polarity; light/dark, good/evil and of course masculine/feminine. In order for us to experience ourselves we must have contrast and that contrast begins with masculine and feminine aspects.

The masculine energy is one of moving forward, outward exploration, colonization, conquering and structure, both literal in buildings and theoretical with rules.

The feminine energy is one of family, balance, inward exploration, equality, inclusivity and a sense of fairness for all. The feminine energy is about exploring who we are and seeking higher meaning in a harmonic way.

At this point, you may be thinking, "Hold on there Patricia! I'm a guy and I care about family and fairness." Or conversely, "Hey there! I'm a woman and I'm the breadwinner. In fact, I'm an engineer so I do go out and build things with rules and whatnot. You aren't making sense!" To which I reply, remember what was stated earlier. We are exploring possibilities based on masculine and feminine versus society's definition of male and female.

Given that we are all spiritual beings, Sparks of One Divine Light, then we all have All That Is within each of us. We can present as a woman with female genitalia and also have balance of masculine and feminine energy within us. It is our mostly patriarchal society that says there are boxes to check for male and female which nature very much does not agree with. In nature everyone does everything in order to survive. Consider Empire Penguins where the male stands guard over the egg through harsh winds while the female goes off to bring home the proverbial bacon. I highly doubt there is any penguin bullying about egg care being the female's job. But I digress...

Imagine, for a moment, a world where there is no gender-based rule for what passions we pursue. Imagine a world where everyone loves freely without bias based on the ability to procreate. Imagine a world where people can live a life fueled by imagination, creativity and passion. Imagine a world where no established process is off limits for improvement. Imagine a world where the decision of whether to pursue an activity is evaluated from multiple points of view and a balanced outcome is decided upon.

Imagine a world not driven by control and instead driven by inclusivity and harmony where everyone not only survives but thrives together. This is the world these children are imagining. This is why they are our hope for a better future. They see a better tomorrow. They don't accept the belief that we must always do what we have always done because we always have. They ask questions; they imagine what would happen if...and then they go out and DO IT! Are they always successful? No. Is every idea brilliant? No. Are some of the concepts and inventions life altering? Yes! Yes! YES!!

"I believe that children are our future. Teach them well and let them lead the way."

Whitney was right. The greatest love of all is inside each of us. If we learn to love ourselves and give ourselves that sense of pride, then we move forward with love and acceptance beaming all around us. Our light paves the way for our journey and lights the way for others. Our joy is infectious, and a world filled with joy would not seek to dominate and destroy. A world filled with joy seeks only to find more joy. When I am engulfed with laughter, I do not seek sadness. I seek out more amusement so the laughter can continue.

Humanity and its continuance depend upon a combined effort of all to live in harmony with the planet. Children come into this world knowing Love and seeing the beauty all around them. It is up to those of us who have been here longer to show them what exists and then listen to their ideas of how it could be better.

We must be careful not to quell them into submission but to encourage them to provide their wisdom. We all have the ability to connect to a higher source within ourselves which again connects to a combined higher source of all souls interwoven. Children come in with that line of communication still intact with full service and unlimited long distance; let them use it. Let them lead the way. Tell them what is in existence without limiting their belief in what is possible.

Children are to be seen and heard. Children are our future literally and figuratively as they have the youth, energy and imagination to find new ways of being. They are not prejudiced against their masculine and feminine traits, therefore using them fully and in complimentary ways. Our job is to nurture them without squelching the seeds of new ideas within their hearts and minds.

Slow down, listen, consider what they say and allow them to come to this life to live the prime directive: explore, experience polarity, find or create harmony and return to unity through Love of all that exists.

Children are our future…. let them lead the way.

Patricia's insights: Children in this context refers to those under the age of 18.

This channel was unusual for me as it seemed to be from my own higher consciousness and my team rather than straight from the team. The tone is closer to my normal speech than some of the others. It seems to me the more I reach out, the harder it is to separate myself from "them".

The idea of masculine energy might offend some people. The masculine label came about purely due to the association with men. Another way of describing this energy would be the explorer, warrior, analytical or controller. These attributes can manifest in either a man or a woman but are valued in the stereotypical man. On the flip side feminine energy would be described as nurturing, spiritual, emotional and loving.

I believe that failure is our best teacher and a lot of the establishment fears failure above all. They would rather succeed at being ineffectual than possibly fail at something innovative.

WHAT DOES THE WORLD MOST NEED TO KNOW RIGHT NOW?

There are so many lonely hearts in the world today. Now, more than ever before, people believe they are alone in the worst ways. There are people who spend their days behind a keyboard or locked behind a closed door, afraid of what the outside world might bring in the way of terror and harm. The world feels like an angry place for far too many people right now. Why is that? What has changed?

People have forgotten who they truly are. They believe that they are just flesh and blood. They believe they have one life to live and that they must fight each other for their piece of the pie. They have forgotten the divinity that lies within their hearts. They have forgotten what they came here to do and who they truly are.

We are all sparks of one divine light of love and creation. We came here with the freedom to choose to live our lives in any way we wished. We came here through the river of forgetfulness so that we could be spiritual beings having a human experience. We forgot that we were born of pure love and light. We came here to experience polarity so that we could experience heaven and hell, light and dark, good and bad. We came here with the ability to be the creators of our existence, to learn and then return to love.

So many have forgotten about love. They have fallen into the belief that the world is a harsh and lonely place. They don't remember that they create their reality and it is only lonely because they have chosen it to be so.

Everything we are, everything we see and all that we encounter exists because we made it so. We came here to understand what a lack of light could look like. We forgot that we control the switch and can brighten the room anytime with a simple change of heart.

A day can be good or bad just because you say it is so. A rainy day can be the devastation of your plans or refreshment of all that you see; nature's way of washing the dust off. It is all in our choosing. Free Will makes it so.

There are always stories of people who have lived through devastation and rose again to become a thriving artist, family member or entrepreneur. They choose to find a way back to the life they want through their actions and belief in something better.

We are all creators of our lives and our experiences. When we allow lower vibration beliefs to inhabit our systems, we fall in energy; creating traps of low vibration and dark energy in our bodies.

Our bodies are created with a will to live and be healthy. Our hearts beat automatically, and our lungs crave sweet, fresh air. Our bodies want to live, we fight to stay alive. When we choose to hang on to worry, fear, doubt and unhealthy beliefs, we create stagnancy where illness breeds. This is not to throw blame upon those who experience illness, but to give hope that they can find the lesson in the situation and then choose to move on from it.

Patricia's insights: The question that was not asked but answered here is why do we fear? This was another time where the message came through me and sounds like me. Personally, I believe that as I merge with my higher self, the transmission gets easier which in turn makes it harder to tell the difference between my team and me.

WHO AM I TO TEACH IF I AM STILL LEARNING?

Oh, dear one! The biggest hope for humanity is that you all come together to help each other. You like the idea of each soul being like a (facet of a) mirror ball, where you all see the world from a slightly different angle. The only way for all of you to see the whole picture full circle is to share each point of view.

In the disco, the ball turns slowly on its axis. Does the perspective of the front door hold less value than the view of the bar? The dance floor? NO! All views assist in showing the full picture. All views have value and the telling of all the stories provides the fascination of life. Fascination stokes the fires of curiosity that leads the individual to want to learn more. Learning more and sharing with others expands the view. Finding that you see the same things and feel similar emotions helps people relate.

As author Lyssa Royal Holt/Germaine said, "The prime directive is to experience polarity and find the way back to unity."

We are one. We are the ball of light before the fracture. The cracks are what make us believe we are alone. Communication and communion of energy help us re-member and realize we are all in fact, connected. All matter. All perspectives have value and sharing along the way helps to ensure a complete picture. Some have the gift to inspire others and to keep that gift hidden is a shame. Jewels of knowledge, just like precious stones, only show the depth of their beauty and value when held up to the light for all to see.

Patricia's insights: Re-member refers to the fact that we believe we are separate and alone when we come into this earth and forget we are all connected. The definition of member is a person, animal, plant, group, etc., that is part of a society, party, community or other body. Therefore, to "remember" would be to come back to that understanding that we are all one.

Essentially to view the teacher as superior or further along is incorrect. The teacher is simply the one who has the information that another lacks. The roles of student or teacher are defined purely by the subject matter.

I do not view myself as an expert on any of this information, I am a student of life. My spirit of intent in sharing what I know is a hope to inspire curiosity.

WHAT DOES HUMANITY MOST NEED TO KNOW IN ORDER TO FEEL HOPEFUL?

What the world needs now is love, sweet love. They weren't wrong back then and they aren't wrong today. The bulk of humanity suffers from a lack of self-love. When we don't love ourselves, we spend all of our energy trying to prove that we are lovable. On top of that we stack the need to be more lovable than the next person. There is a real focus on competition and the need to be better than someone else, instead of just better than the person we were yesterday.

There is a lack of love. Loving oneself silences that inner critic who extinguishes our greatest desires and denies our gifts. We have all come here with contributions to make to humanity. Without your contribution, the recipe is missing something; a key ingredient that leaves the dish slightly off. I am important, you are important. He, she, they are ALL as important as the next person. Now if you are reading this and you are thinking well that person over there is not as important as me because… (fill in the blank,) you are missing the point. You are missing the love of yourself. You don't need them to be less for you to be more, being yourself is enough. It is actually very simple. Humanity makes it complex. It need not be.

We have free will. We can choose to feel love or choose something else. If I am worried about how it sounds to the next person, I need to add in more self-love. If I love myself fully and completely, another's opinion won't matter. I can just be love, without worrying about someone else's opinion and if, in fact, they are just busy filling themselves with love then it just gets better and better.

Have you ever been in that honeymoon state where you just love everybody and everything around you? Do you notice that when you go out into the world in that state of mind that good things happen to you? Maybe someone lets you go in front of them in a busy market line. Or maybe the waiter comps your dessert. That's what love does. It gives back to you manifold.

If you have "tried love in the past" and it hasn't worked out, I'd be willing to bet you were giving love externally before applying that self-love internally. We need to fill our own tanks before we can supply the rest of the world. No one will love you more than you love yourself. You cannot give the love you don't have inside, no matter how hard you try.

So truly, what the world needs now is love, sweet love. All you need to do is love yourself. That begins with accepting yourself just as you are today, right here, right now. Not 10 pounds lighter or $10 dollars richer. Right flat out now. As is, no warranties or discounts applied. Just love you. Full on, in the state you are in today. Right now. This second.

It may take some time. "You mean I have to love myself with that wart on my knee and that wrinkle on my face?" Yes!

"I have to love myself even though I yelled at my postman and cut that guy off in traffic?" Yes.

Forgive yourself for not living up to your own standards. Send yourself love and move on to a better decision next time. Moment to moment, love you no matter where you are at.

It is hard, but then, it is really not hard. You know? Be honest. The only reason you don't love yourself all the time is because society tells you that's not ok. You must be conceited or narcissistic. It's not the same. Loving yourself at the expense of others is one thing. Loving yourself where you are at right now is the thing we are talking about. You, right there, right now, in that chair, reading this note. You are perfect. You are the best you can be in this moment in time doing something good for yourself in reading about how you can and should love yourself as you are. So, you are doing fine. You aren't doing another person harm. You are doing good for you. Stop. Just breathe for a moment. Connect with your heart. Send love from you to you. Feels good doesn't it?

Start small. Three long, slow, deep breaths once in the morning and once in the evening sending love from you to you. The more you do this, the better you feel. The better you feel, the better you behave. The better you behave, the better interactions you have with others. When they ask what you are doing, you can tell them, or you can tell them to go and read this for themselves. Your call. No pressure.

WITH THE STATE OF THE PLANET TODAY AND ALL THE CHANGES THAT WE SEE, HOW CAN PEOPLE BE SO BLISSFULLY UNAWARE OF OUR IMPACT ON THE WORLD? OR IF CONFRONTED WITH THINGS WE CAN EACH DO, HOW CAN THEY BE SO CALLOUS AS TO SAY THINGS LIKE "IT WON'T HAPPEN IN MY LIFETIME"? HOW CAN I HAVE HOPE WHEN IT SEEMS THE WORLD IS SO FULL OF SELFISH AND CARELESS PEOPLE?

Oh, my dear, one we feel your pain and we see the worry lines on your face. You need not fear. The world will not end. Mother Earth has seen this before and she will survive. Your brothers and sisters are all at different stages in their awakening. It is hard for you to stand there and listen and take in all that they are saying. We know the ignorance of their words hurts your heart and you are not alone. The readers of this book will be the same. They will wonder at the slim chance they see of the world waking up in time to do something for humanity and for the planet.

There are two things to consider here. One is the planet. As we have said before, the planet will be fine. It will change and grow and recover. Species will adapt to the changes in the weather. Flocks will migrate as the temperate zones move around and the Earth will, in time, cover mankind's mistakes of the cemented cities.

Each human will survive or perish based on the decisions they make. Your spirit will go on. You, reading this now and the one originally asking the question, know this to be true in the depths of their heart. Humans will go on to see the error of their ways and the good or bad they have done. They will see where they could have done things differently and will feel the cause and effect of the decisions they made. Life will go on. The spirit will go on.

How, you ask, can so many be blind to what you see as obvious with your plain sight? It is because they are not looking with clear vision. Their view is obscured by their egos, the desires of their baser selves and worldly distractions. They are still in the mindset of the possessive nature of the masculine structure of the world.

Humanity is changing, yes. Many are awakening to the ways of a unified view but many, as yet, are also not ready. They cannot see what is right in front of them as if their eyes are indeed closed.

The sadness you feel is the dissonance between your heart that is open and pure and the hearts of those who are still boxed up in a world that is ruled by closed minds. Logic can find an argument to the pure and clear truth that the eyes would see. If one does not desire to understand the truth of a situation then they will find a way to justify their position allowing them to carry on as they wish.

This is the choice of Free Will. It is something that we will not step in to change. As you, the one originally asking the question, have recently learned, the prime directive of the earthly mission for humanity is to experience polarity. How could you have the honest experience of that if we were to step in and course correct you every few miles? That would not be an honest ride for you dear traveller. You must take the wheel and set your own course on this adventure. Just as the driver and the passenger will see different things along the way, so shall two people who live side by side experience the world differently. It is all ok, it is all good and exactly as it is to be.

The pain you feel is the memory from previous lives where humanity has made the same mistakes and perhaps even times where you were in the other seat, seeing things through the eyes of technology and science, rather than with the lens of the heart showing you what is happening without filters.

It is okay. It is good. It is as it should be for the lessons to be learned. The changes will come when enough of you are ready. In the meantime, you can speak to the ears that are ready to hear and in some you may find deafness, or an unwillingness to part with the point of view that serves them. It is not for you to decide the way of the many. It is for you to act upon your own wishes and desires, trusting that your fellow man will also find their way.

If not, then you will try again as is the way of the lessons of the division into polarities.

Dear one, we know the words of those who refuse to make small changes to advance the whole of humanity hurts your heart. We know it confuses and confounds you, but you must have trust. You must trust that all who need to are also doing their parts, even if you cannot see them. You must trust that the influence you have in the ears of those who would hear you, is enough. You must gently lead through your own actions and choices and try, when you can, to influence in a gentle and loving way. You must work on the need to judge and accept that all are one and one is in all. As enough of you make the change, all of you will make the change and humanity shall have a victory over itself.

Love is always the answer no matter what. Even in your confoundedness over the words and actions of those who you thought you knew; you must trust and love and just wait. Work on yourself and those around you will benefit as well, you are all part of the one.

We cannot say that enough. You are all part of the one so

changes you make for yourself do indeed influence and impact the whole of the web.

Love, love, love and then love some more. That is the way. That is the light and that is the answer to the problem you experience.

Patricia's insights: For the world to move forward, we need to move forward with a balance of science and spirituality. We need to have less judgment and need to be right. Rather than responding with "that's stupid" it would be better to say, "That's an interesting observation. Let's explore it."

There is tendency in western society to value the mind over the gut and heart. We can have a gut feeling about something that we then rationalize away in order to go with the flow, giving in to peer pressure. In my opinion, we are better served by learning to listen with our hearts, guts and minds without judgment; being truer to ourselves.

WHAT EFFECT WILL OUR MATURITY IN OUR EMOTIONS HAVE ON OUR COMPASSION FOR HUMANITY?

The Light of Orion was called in to answer this question.

Emotions are a complex thing that we have embedded to enhance the experience of the planet. That can be a tool or a weapon in our understanding of the events that surround us. We cannot grow to a place of complete acceptance if we do not harness our emotions to guide them to loving interactions and away from fear and judgment. It is okay to be different than the next person. It is okay for one person to see the world differently than another. As you have suggested, dear one who asked the question, it is the judgment that is the key to removal of the negative emotion. We only need to accept one another where the other is at and not sit in our high and mighty seat of judgment against them. All is as it should be for the other person. Our role is to enact the emotion of loving-kindness in all situations. To go to judgment is to create a situation of right versus wrong. The versus is unnecessary. All choices have validity; all experiences are necessary. If you wish to influence someone to choose loving-kindness, you will not achieve that goal through deeming them to be wrong.

The planet is growing in its maturity by the choices that each individual makes in each moment and each and every interaction with one another. Righteousness has had its time on earth and now it is time for that to be done. This is not a judgment (laughs) in itself, but a fact. You may choose whatever you wish but you don't need to make another's choice wrong in relation to your choice. Acceptance. Love. Kindness. Patience. Joy. Friendship. Allowance for differences of opinion. Each person must choose their experience and each person must experience the outcome of their choice. Do not judge. Observe and notice the outcomes of the choices without losing the love in your heart for the other. They are you and you are they and by them choosing differently than you, you may not have to make that choice in order to get the lesson. Thank them for their service to humanity, as you are witnessing the outcome of their choices from afar.

The emotion of compassion would be in place if you view their experience through the lens of loving-kindness. Send them the emotion of love and acceptance from your heart center. The feeling is pure good and high in energy whereas the lower emotion of judgment is not of high vibration.

So, don't judge the judges; simply observe, make note and carry on with your loving ways. You are doing well, and you are doing good by simple and silent observance. Your actions are the key to influence others. They will see the peace in your face, feel the love emanate from your heart and wonder how you became so. The quiet influence is more powerful than the shouting indignation of a judge.

Carry on gentle soul. Your path is bringing you joy. Love is the answer. We love you; we see you; we appreciate your journey. Always.

HOW DO WE GET FROM THE PRESENT REALITY TO THE REALITY OF COMPASSIONATE LOVE IN OUR THOUGHTS AND ACTIONS IN EVERYDAY LIFE?

We hear you asking, "How do we get from a state of separation and self centeredness to a state of love, acceptance, and compassion for our fellow man?" Yes? This is the state that you desire, that we desire, that is the desirable state. Oh, dear one, there is so much love available to us that we are capable of accessing and sharing amongst all God's creatures great and small if only we choose it. It is in fact a choice to love. There is love and there isn't anything else. That is all. We make it so difficult and it need not be so. Yet that is the grand design of free will. What happens if I choose love? More love happens. What happens if I want a more dramatic experience? More drama occurs. There was at time when all the souls were young and wanted to take the path of (most) resistance, to experience all the challenges of a human life. The chaos has become a choice of so many that the chaos is what we mostly see while love hides in the corners. It is time for the love to pour out all of the cracks and the crannies. Open the doors of your hearts wide and shine the love. When your heart calls out with love, the signal is heard, and hearts call back. The essence of every single thing you see here; every pebble is made from the seed of love. All the vibrations that create everything on earth are all seeded from love. So, when you call out with that love from the reservoir of your heart, all the world responds. The echo of the memory of the love calls back.

HOW LONG WILL THIS TAKE? HOW CAN WE POSSIBLY SOLVE ALL THE CHAOS THAT EXISTS TODAY?

It takes the time it takes, and we are not ones to consider your earthly time. Are you asking if there is enough time? Yes, time is a human construct as we have said in the past, you can not and will not run out of something that only exists in the minds of humans. We are infinite and as are you. Well then, all is infinite, so yes, there is enough of this human "time" to save everything. There is no saving to be done, only choosing. Choosing to follow our hearts and to trust that love is strong enough to overcome all else that has been created. The how is the trust of a heart of a child. The child still feels the love and sees the smallest offering of love and focuses on that to grow the entire experience of a person from the spark of love. The child sees the good in another over the other views. The child brings out the love in the hardest of hearts and grows it into an entire experience of a person. Does this make sense, dear one?

Even where the spark of love in a hardened heart is just a whisper of what used to be. The innocent ones see and recognize, feel and experience that whisper of love. They fan the flame with their smiles and giggles and goos and silly antics to grow the heart flame into love. This is the key. Love with the heart of that child that you see, that child who you were when you came here to this place, before you forgot who you were - who you ALL are. We are all love and we return to love. We have said this before. If you choose love, you cannot go wrong.

In your books you say, sometimes in jest, "What would Jesus do?" Well Jesus was love incarnate. So really you are asking, "What would love do? If my choices are many and I choose with a loving heart, what would that choice be?" If all make the choice of how to act and how to proceed with the question what would love do, all will be returning to love.

We know this sounds simple; some might say it sounds like a child's viewpoint of simplicity. And to that we say YES, a resounding booming warm and joyous YES! It is simple. It is child's play because the child who you were knew the answer was love. The adult forgot. Return to love. Choose love. BE LOVE. The answer is love; it truly is, dear ones.

CHAPTER 4

LOVE, SURRENDER, TRUST, AND THEN ACTION

Action

by Ann and Bill
as part of Team Love

We, Ann and Bill, provide this format for you, as the human and the soul, to understand that what we share is not outside ourselves, or yourselves, for that matter. What we have is all inside ourselves, but it requires choice. Choice of action towards love to embody that which we already are, love. What will you choose?

As we came together on April Fool's Day, 2012, we chose to step into love not knowing where it would take us or how it would unfold. We were simply taking action. This book is a reflection of our journey as it comes in both the human and non-human forms for us thus far. They are one in the same.

In this book we will share both the broader "Team" perspective and each of our own perspectives on hope for humanity through love. As part of this chapter, Ann will also share an audio version of an ancient Galactic Language that your soul will understand, even if you cannot through the human mind.

As part of the purchase of this book, we have provided the audio links for you to listen to of that language, in order to help you absorb what it is we truly wish to share at a soul level. Excerpts can be listened to in conjunction with, or as an add on, to each section that we have created. At any point simply go to the following hyperlink – https://loveevolution.ca/hope-audios

LET'S START WITH THE QUESTION OF WHY THE TITLE "HOPE FOR HUMANITY"?

The Team begins with an example, or an analogy, to ponder. When a child is lost in the woods the child becomes very frightened. In fact, that child would do things that a child would normally not do - it would take chances and perceive things in the forest based on fear. However, if you walked up to that child and said, "Beyond the stream and beyond the trees is what you seek," the child would change before your very eyes and believe there is a possibility that he/she could get to where he/she innately knows he/she was seeking to go.

Humanity is often considered to be children seeking their direction as part of an experience, or experiment. It is this time on your planet, where there are many beings that are whispering in the child's ear. Some are saying things like, "Look in the trees young ones. See the scary creatures." And then there are others that are saying, "Keep doing what you need to do. Turn to the right. Turn to the right."

When a child is lost, they are open to many messages. They are open to many directions that do not produce hope. They produce false delusions of forward momentum. The title of this book is to bring about the true knowing within you, but not knowing with your mind. It is knowing with your heart that humanity has an increasing opportunity for transformation. But the most important part is that it starts with you carrying hope for humanity.

You see it is through love being lived in your world that brings about the hope you see. When that child is told that just beyond the trees is the home he/she seeks, what does it do emotionally? It puts them into a different state, the physical body changes you will find that love exudes from them. They are willing to accept, you see, that they are worthy of making it home. Just as you will feel that in reading these excerpts, that there is hope for you through love, and by being on this planet you help change it and create hope.

Ann's perspective: This is how I felt when I met Bill on April Fool's Day, 2012, and when we began working with the embodiment technologies which we have been graced with, and the community we have found around the globe. There was more space for love. I could step more easily into being me. That which I know I already am but kept finding it difficult to be each and every day in this human form. You see we carry so many stories of what we are not, all based on fear, that we, in this human form, struggle to stay consistently in this space, the space of love and neutrality that we truly are. If we understood who we truly are, there would be no struggle, no fear, and no lack; we would just be.

That certainly was not my life before I connected with

Bill and The Team through love. Once we met there was a ray of hope and there was no stopping me. I was like a locomotive on steroids looking for love, getting back to that which I knew I am but had somehow lost along the way. Like a child looking for love, this was an inner knowing. One that I knew I must follow to the end.

My soul knew, I knew, it was a matter of choice. I have discovered true freedom - it lies in embodying who we truly are, LOVE.

Listen to Ann's light language perspective on "Why Hope for Humanity" at https://loveevolution.ca/hope-audios

Bill's Perspective: I completely agree with Ann's perspective. For me, this journey started with the shift from wondering to knowing. When I look back, I would never have anticipated the journey that has taken place over the last decade. It has been about surrendering and taking action.

At the time I didn't understand what I was about to do. It all started with a group sound event in Colorado and I still remember it well. I was laying on the floor, relaxing, listening to the crazy frequencies that were being played, when something so small created such a change in my destiny. Since then, I've had the opportunity with Ann in my life, to work, meet, talk, speak, channel, and communicate with literally thousands of people. It all started with that change, that change from wondering to knowing, the change from buying a lottery ticket on life, versus having the winning ticket. You see if you won $10 million tomorrow, your whole life wouldn't change instantly. However, over the coming days, weeks and months your whole perspective of what is important and what is not important gradually changes.

For example, you might change what type of car you drive or what type of house you live in. This is really what happened to me. Once I had knowingness that I was safe, my life became a wonderful expression of getting over myself and having some fun. Once I knew this, gradually my world unfolded. Is it easy like so many spiritual people say? NOPE. Sometimes it can be fucking hard. Is it worth it? Absolutely, completely, 100% yes, yes, yes and more YES. For me, the question right from the beginning was, if I let go, if I truly let go and surrender and allow, what will my life be?

Well, it starts with a step. It might be reading this book. It might be listening to some of the communications. Mine started with choosing love as the outcome for my life. That's what I (we) ask you to do. Choose love for your life, and the journey will change gradually and dramatically, since it has the potential to bring you into alignment with what is possible for your soul.

TAKING ACTION TOWARDS CHANGE THROUGH LOVE AND SURRENDER

The Team begins with another example. One day, the clothing designer wakes up and has a vision of creating this beautiful dress. She goes into the fabric store and sees all the beautiful fabrics. Then she feels a few of them, to feel whether they come into her image of the reality she wants to create. She is assembling components to a vision that she's had. She purchases, or is gifted, whatever is the approach in this vision of hers, goes home and begins to create the pattern that she envisioned. Oh yes, she goes through a few little mistakes and fixes them and continues her journey of creating what she saw. This example is to remind you that having the vision, as this beautiful clothing designer had, is not enough. How did this being create something in this dimension that you find yourselves in? By taking action.

In this quantum space that you find yourself in, there is a movement of change coming. However, it is not the movement of a few, it is a movement of the many. If you are reading, listening, and participating in this exchange, you are already in the mode of considering or are in a state of movement. Many say thinking about it brings about the reality, we say of course that does help, but taking action amplifies it significantly. During the time you find yourself in now, approximately 37 more years, there is a maximum amplification or possibility when you take action.

Look at your life. Go inside and do a little review. How many times have you found yourself wishing and thinking that things could be and should be different for you, but you didn't take action? You merely sit and watch your life pass by. You don't believe. You don't have hope that your small action could bring about the change for you. So many in your world are unhappy in relationships, are unhappy in abundance, are unhappy with where they live.

Through this book, one of the intentions is for you to understand that there is hope and then take action. It does not mean that you have to end relationships or anything so dramatic, unless you choose. That is your choice. However, remember you make a difference.

Without action you do make some difference, of course; however, if you are willing to step into action, you multiply the effects hundreds and hundreds of times over. If you are willing to take action through love, then the world really does change for you. It changes inside first. Then, the inside begins to change the outside; one person affects the next person. The question becomes, "Are you worthy, as a child, to take a step towards home? Are you worthy as the clothing designer, to take a step by going out of the comfort of your own reality to move into the flow of building the dream, of getting home, or creating the beauty?" It is your choice. These words are merely meant to remind you there is hope. There is hope for humanity. And you, the reader, are the hope.

Ann's perspective: This is what I have done everyday since I realized there was more to life worth living than the traditional confines that I had built in my first 40 plus years on this planet. What I was seeking didn't lie with what I did know but instead with what I didn't know.

So, I too, like you, began seeking. Taking action, through love, taking action towards the inner knowing that what I was seeking existed inside of me. It was waiting to be rebirthed and reformed through the eyes of love. I was not willing to follow others, I wanted to lead my own change through love.

Listen to Ann's light language perspective here
on "Taking Action Towards Change Through
Love" at https://loveevolution.ca/hope-audios

Bill's perspective: This example I want to give might make more sense to people that are, let us say, a little more immersed in the technology side of the world. But either way, it's of tremendous value to me to look back to the days of the dot-com era.

I had a vision and a partnership with a friend, and together we raised money and put it towards a project. However, when I look back now, the whole foundation for the project was based on greed. It was based on getting the investors and us to make money. And now here lies an opportunity in my life with Ann, where once again I am co-creating something completely unique on the planet, as was the case in the dot-com era. This time, however, everything is being done through the eyes of love. It's a completely different business model.

Being the entrepreneur and computer technologist for over 40 years, this is a very different way of perceiving a reality that in some way we can conduct business based on loving exchanges. We can create products that are about loving experiences. We can even create distribution models based on integrity, honesty and fairness. So, the whole project that we are looking at in the moment, and you may hear about in the future, is about doing this differently. As Ann said, through the eyes of love.

There's a possibility on this planet that we will be able to conduct commerce and exchange energy movement in a fair, open, and loving way. I've watched spiritual communities and some beings do exactly that, but very few. There's still the mentality rooted in our culture of "What's in it for me?" that we forget to just allow love to flow. There's no reason why finances and abundance cannot be singing in harmony with love. That's the hope for humanity.

It's not about destroying our earth. It's about transforming it through the eyes of love. Even what I do on the keyboard when I'm creating programs is done with an eye towards helping to build, and support a richer more abundant loving life, for individuals, families and their communities. It all started when I decided to take more and more action. Did I know 10 years ago that I would literally be sitting in a car dictating this portion of the book? I had no fucking idea. None. Zero. Would I have thought that I would create a product to help humanity through love? Well, I had those dreams as a child when I was four and five. I saw many things that you can now buy in the store, but I never took action. I was told I couldn't do it. I wasn't capable enough.

Ann and I are now choosing to take action without knowing what the outcome will be. We are fully trusting and surrendering. We will create ripples in our and other's realities, allowing you to see the hope and be inspired to take your own loving action.

AWAKENING TO LOVE

The Team's perspective: Choices, choices, and more choices. Sometimes you as a human get overwhelmed by choices. The media can influence your choices trying to get you to make a certain decision in all aspects of your life. Even the non-physicals in this communication have choices. The Team speaking to you do not have to help humanity. There is no obligation. It is choice. Your soul does not have to seek to provide you with an abundant, fun, and exciting life. You do not "have to" be open. You do not "have to" connect to the higher being that you are. There is no "have to"; it is your choice. You do not "have to" believe there is hope for humanity. It is your choice. You do not "have to" step into fear. That is your choice. As a human, this universe was created with two simple polarities, and that is enough complexity for the human mind.

There are other planetary systems where there are many more polarities such as love and fear. Where do you choose to spend your time and energy? You are this vast being that has access to many lives simultaneously. You have access to much messaging and yet a huge percentage of humans on your planet choose fear, hatred and destruction. The little child that was lost in the woods got to this point because he/she chose to move through the woods to try to find home. That child made a choice – to awaken to love.

Humanity is now at a point to make a choice – love, joy or peace. Many speak of ascension and vibration. This language is fine but what do you, the reader, the perceiver of the reality choose, when you are hearing, feeling, or reading these words? Are you choosing to see the world as a place of love? Are you choosing to see yourself as being capable of love and in fact being willing to take a step towards existing and transmitting love? Throughout the chapters you will find various beings challenging you through their stories and communications and encouraging you to make the choice to be conscious of what you are doing with your energy.

You see, even the non-physicals never sit in judgment of you, for you have chosen to participate in a human experience where you get and have been given, the sovereignty to make your own choice. We merely encourage you to be conscious of your choices. If you find you need to seek outside assistance to help you wake up, then choose and take action. Choice without action leaves the child standing saying, "I want to turn to the right." The child wants to make a choice that he/she will go to the right, then the child must turn to the right or the choice means nothing in his/her life. Now there is some value, but you have been drawn to this communication because you are seeking to make choices. You are seeking to believe that there is hope for you, and through that, there is hope for humanity.

You are capable of changing you and through this is the change you see, believe and feel that is required for humanity. Is there hope? We would simply remind you, are you willing to believe? Are you willing to have hope for yourself? We understand that you made a choice by reading these words. In this is the beginning of the action that can spiral the waves that can move you forward. Is it just a simple read of a chapter? The answer is YES. Because not only did you make a choice, you took action. Through that there will be peace, calmness and love, giving you the framework to simply move forward, make a choice, take action, and step into love.

Ann's perspective: So that is what I did when I met Bill and the divine sciences that spoke to my soul on April 1, 2012. I remembered that I was capable of more, so much more than I could remember. So, I took action. I went to a group, did a session, bought a technology and then dedicated my life and the life of my partner to each other's evolution through love. What do you choose? What action will you take through love today?

Listen to Ann's light language perspective here
on "Awakening to Love" at
https://loveevolution.ca/hope-audios

Bill's perspective: If you would have told me all the steps and all the things that would transpire in my life since that moment in Colorado and even since Ann and I came together, as a senior analyst, I would've fired you for being delusional. That would be just absolute 'crazy talk' and yet here we are.

Oh my God, the crazy experiences Ann and I have had. Friendships, love, intimacies, experiences, travel and yes, some of them were disappointing. When you're in the old way, we would think that loving someone is about allowing them to do whatever they want in relationship to us, because that's what we thought was loving. Then a few years ago, Ann and I both came to this deep understanding that unconditional love is not about taking it on the chin. If you're in a position in your life where you're, you know, taking it on the chin so to speak, then we would encourage you to look inside, decide and tell me or tell yourself how is that loving?

So, the journey has been about awakening to an inner potential, awakening to an inner strength. I've typically been rather a gentle person. It is my disposition in this life, but I also used to just take it on the chin and never voiced what I thought was important. I don't do that any longer. I stand up for what I believe is correct and accept that you might not agree, and that's fine. What holds the fabric of my existence together is surrendering.

As I look at my life, the old sequence of logic that I used to use in building large systems and planning old IT projects has completely gone. Now it just seems that the most important thing is to take action. You don't have to wait until you have it perfect. Just fucking do it. As soon as you take a step, it seems like what you used to think was perfect is no longer perfect. Just allow, unfold, let go, and love. That friend that you've never said I love you to? Do it. Just take action based on this principle of love. This journey is about love and I am so grateful for Ann in my life and so grateful that you're reading this chapter because it is about sharing this love with you. Now is the time to take action.

THE ROLE OF SELF LOVE

The Team's Perspective: You see, when a person is on a journey of love, there will come a time, where the mind says things like, "Why? What is this all about? My heart, the love I am, I have had enough for this life. For my social circumstances, my life needs time to catch up." The next phase is about bringing the soul energy into you. It is not about you reaching for it. What does this do to the human? When you allow it, it is unconditional, joy, happiness and bliss. It is times like this that the ego often lays claim to it being the part of your existence and has created the situations to allow you to be in joy, happiness, bliss, focus and concentration, all of these wonderful attributes of being human.

It is also at this stage that 99.9% of beings become derailed. For when these enhanced states of consciousness are brought about through an integration of a small percentage of more of your soul energy, the ego tries to create stories about how this activity, that activity or this person or this sexual experience or this intimacy moment is related to joy. Because of the ego, because of the thinking mind, there's a relationship made to the joy. When you create this mind relationship to joy and happiness, then the mind is continually put upon to try to recreate the situation of love in action.

As you move forward, loving yourself becomes one of the most key areas of acceleration for you. This is only to be sustainable when one is in love and comfortable with oneself. Without love of self, the mind is continually trying to decide what is wrong with itself. Why are you feeling very calm and at peace in the middle of people fighting and yelling at each other, as an example? In this state of remaining calm, you will have demonstrated that you have a capacity to love you. You have a capacity, to stay neutral as you observe what is happening. This next stage of expansion or entrainment is about you being able to exist in a state of happy consciousness. This is love. You are able to exist in a state of complete love of self and love of others. It is only through the complete surrender to the experience of love that you will be able to maintain this state.

As you step into different states of awareness, consciousness, and integration of love, new patterns around your being open up. What you used to think was your "dream relationship", let us use that language, the "dream woman", so to speak, the "dream job", when you open to deeper states of love, all of a sudden change happens.

Imagine driving your car in through the city and you can only turn the steering wheel half a turn. You will be limited to what you get to experience and see. Then, all of a sudden, your steering gets more and more and more expansive. What you couldn't see before now becomes a different reality of existence, and yet for you to be able to explain it to an individual that has not surrendered, allowed love to flow, is almost impossible in the human world. You are only able to show it. Explaining it is not necessary. The most important thing is living love, letting go of your preconceptions of what love must be, and letting go of your patterns of how you need to interact with other humans.

Ann's perspective: For so many years I chose to love others but not myself. My belief was that love of others, love of my husband, love of my children, and love of my family was all I needed. But inside I knew I was not being true to me. We are so conditioned in the human form to believe that self love is selfish, love is dirty, love is unkind, or love needs to be a certain way or experienced/ expected in a certain way. So, we turn it off inside ourselves, we give up hope. Because we know the truth; love is none of those things. Until we are willing to let go of what we believe love should or should not be, we will never find our way back home. Nine years of "looking for love" now knowing it was all inside me if I was willing to embody it and be the REAL me, not the me others expected, not the role of mother, father, sister - the real me. Years of undoing other people's stories to find the real me and this journey will never stop. That is love; that is self-love, like no other exists on this planet. Now what to do with that love is yet to be seen.

If I can help you begin to understand by sharing in this book, that you are not what you think, then I have done my job. I have shown that undoing what is not love is well worth the ride. Love of self, undoing the false illusions, not loving others, is what drives this awakening within our soul to reconnect to the love within our human form.

Listen to Ann's light language perspective here on "Self-Love Embodied in the Human Form" at https://loveevolution.ca/hope-audios

Bill's perspective: As I sit contemplating what to share about self-love, I realize there are so, so many elements. When I review my life, I realize there are times that, in the moment, I thought I was being self-loving, but I really wasn't. That's an interesting challenge for me. How can I love myself and still live the childhood patterning that was given to me as the preacher's child? For example, I was taught to put others first. It was an interesting challenge for me that I've moved through. Loving yourself is also about an honouring of you. What I mean by this is recognizing that what I do in life, when I love myself, becomes a reflection of me.

So, I understand as a child I had a lot of ideas of things. I loved to make things and create things. However, I went through my life fitting into social patterning by allowing friends to influence what I created or didn't create. I thought I had to go through the structures of life, marriage, and children. I always thought that's what love is, and self-love was merely being an extremely loving and kind person. I'm just realizing now after almost 60 years that the deepest levels of self-love I can provide myself is honouring the innate talents I have, respecting them, and giving myself a chance in this life to live them. When I bottle up my ideas and thoughts that I have inside of my mind, I'm not loving and honouring myself, I'm hiding. When I see someone, I truly love them. So, the question to ask yourself is, am I honouring myself by not letting that person know that they are deeply loved? For me, I honour myself as I honour others through love. When I create something and come up with some crazy idea, it is this deep honouring and loving of self that I create something that I give to others as part of my human experience.

It's actually right now in writing this part of the book that I understand how deeply the pattern seems to run in me, that I deny myself and I deny myself and I deny myself. My commitment in this life, and to my beautiful partner Ann, is to love myself so deeply that I honour all pieces of me. Whether it is hugging and loving people, whether it is creating technologies, whether it is sharing experiences. Holding space for the complete embodiment of love brings about the ability to take action as social conscious beings. That's what we're doing right now. If you saw and had a little window into our lives, it's in the process of huge change. I finally understand it's about me honouring me. So, the question to you is, what parts of your life are you not honouring? What parts of you, your soul, your experiences are you ignoring? How many things do you have piled up or swept under the carpet?

Now you don't have to do it all at once, maybe it's time to take a look just as Ann and I have done by committing to being in this book. Maybe it's time for you to honour you and love yourself.

THE ROLE OF SURRENDER THROUGH LOVE

The Team's Perspective: Your book, Hope for Humanity, comes at a wonderful time in the transition activities we see taking place on earth. Many humans are endeavouring to take steps and move forward using their consciousness and minds to create opportunities and change. Let us say there was a large group of beings endcavouring to change the world. Each of them operating independently and operating on their own thoughts, concepts and translation of what they think they need to do. The challenge to this approach is there is approximately 38% non-alignment of activities. One person tries to move forward and another believes that is not about moving forward to love, not about giving hope for humanity, and so they endeavour to stop the progress of those that are really endeavouring to do and perform in the same way, towards a unified goal.

This is where surrender comes into the mix. Why surrender? Most of you that are reading this book have toyed with this concept. In fact, most of you reading this book refuse to surrender, for in some way, in your mind, surrender is about releasing your capacity to be an individual. You see this is not correct. Surrender is completely the opposite. Let us explain and reiterate what surrender is in this layer of communication to you.

Surrender is about accepting, believing and trusting that you are a higher conscious being in the human form. Surrender comes with many layers and steps. It is about releasing the knowing from your egoic thinking mind.

It does not mean you stop thinking. You have beautiful minds, carry on with life, but begin the process of letting go of thinking you know.

If you were to think that there is a larger consciousness, a larger movement at foot on your world, the answer is yes there is; you are correct. The challenge is that it is not without you. You are part of the movement, the change. However, at a higher level, when you surrender and allow your soul presence into your being, we equate this simply with love. When you allow love to dominate your thoughts, energies, and feelings, what tends to happen with the energy is your ego acquiesces, slows down, goes to sleep and allows you to be. When you are in a state of being. You are in a state of high connection to the soul. As you practice this, you will find that the soul energy will flow strongly through you, and your intuition increases.

Surrendering to love is the reason love is important in surrendering. For example, when you have a thousand people in a large auditorium, and you teach the pattern of surrender, they begin to practice it, but you don't point out that it's surrendering to love. You just say surrender. The challenge with this is you open your consciousness to surrendering to influences. Now, this is not a 100% accurate statement, but when you surrender to love, you are demanding of your consciousness and demanding of the universe through this surrender pattern to only allow the energy of love to flow.

When you surrender to love, you connect very strongly to the soul. As you do this, in relationship to this book, as you create this connection, you get to perceive the world differently. It is this difference that instantly gives you

Hope for Humanity.

Now again, this illustration, we started with a large group of beings endeavouring to make change in your world, it is a percentage of them, and over 38%, are in conflict within themselves. If all those beings surrendered to love, then the vibration and communication would enhance the group. In fact, their souls would be able to communicate between each other, one million times faster than humans are able to communicate to each other. The souls then orchestrate larger movements, more powerful, and more sustainable movements. However, you may have a specific thing that your soul wants you to do. If you stay in surrender to love, you will get the message. Then we implore you, implore upon you, to take action. Keep surrendering to love and then take action. Love, is the uniform energy that is used to communicate whenever the people are brought together to make progress, increase vibration, increase health and to heal people. It is done through the vibration of love. Therefore, when you are surrendered to this mode/practice, you are able to communicate. Have you ever noticed that when your mind goes silent or goes into a state of love, you don't feel alone? For you know as a human and sense as a soul that you are connected to all things.

Now, some call it creator. That is correct. Some call it the divine. That is correct. Some call it connected to their guides. That is correct. Some call it connected to their soul. All of these terms are correct, but they are all predicated on the embodiment of living in love.

It does not mean you have to get up in the morning and stop everything for four hours as you put yourself in

117

a state to surrender to love. Surrendering to love is a way of life. It's a way of living. It is combined with this unknowingness of what is going on, allowing your mind to take a break from believing in what other people are saying is going on. Merely let go of all of it. As you let go, freedom, joy, and love come in. Then if you are willing to stay in this state, throughout the day, you will get inspiration. We suggest 97% of the readers of this book, if you are willing to surrender to love, you will begin to feel a part of something much larger than you, and that is your soul's connection to the universe. This energy of love is what brings positive change on earth. Be at peace.

Ann's perspective: In the beginning of my journey with Bill, I believed I had made choices that I thought were big, but I could not accept the concept of surrender. I believed that somehow surrender was giving up and, man oh man, I was not willing to give up. Surrender in my mind meant that I was giving up hope for me, hope for humanity, hope for love, and dog gone it, I was not giving up on that.

Many times, I would find myself kicking, and screaming, and yelling, as I made a decision to surrender and then it did not turn out the way I had expected. That's not surrender. What I have realized over time is that what I was surrendering was my belief that I could do it all by myself, that I was somehow responsible for something I did not even understand. I could not fathom being part of a team I could not imagine or even see. And yet here I am!

In hindsight, surrendering through love, love of self, love of others has allowed me to more fully step into me, the real me. The being that has always wanted to help make a change through love but did not know how. And what I have learned is that through surrender, and only surrender, I am being shown the real me. Now letting go and surrendering was not so easy for me as the ex-tax accountant from KPMG who prided herself on knowing everything she could. They don't write that shit in the Income Tax Act. But as I practiced surrendering to love more and more, I realized there were more layers of complexity and more layers of letting go. It's like my mind and my ego still wanted control. As I write this section in this book, I realize that even in writing and launching our next initiatives, I do not know. I must trust, trust love, surrender, and then take action.

Listen to Ann's light language perspective here on "Why Surrender to Love?" " at https://loveevolution.ca/hope-audios

Bill's perspective: So, the question is how has surrender played out in my life? As I go through the years, and the visuals flash through my mind in writing this, there are so many pieces of my life that I didn't surrender at first. Instead, I pushed and kept pushing through life, business, and relationships. I disguised it all around the concept that "My word is my bond." If I say, "I'll do it", I'll do it. Even if I kill myself doing it, it doesn't matter. I'll do it. It is the opposite when I review my life instead of surrendering; I took control.

I have a very strong mind. You could call me extremely, excessively stubborn. I admit it. I pretty much had to be dropped to my knees to actually surrender. Since then, in the last 11 years, there are very few days that I don't repeat to myself – I surrender. When I met my beautiful partner Ann, I found myself feeling strange that we had just started this wonderful relationship and I was completely surrendering everything about it. If she chose another partner, I surrendered that. I surrendered her times when she was going through releasing her frustration, anger and sometimes depression.

When I continue to look back, surrender is the biggest gift I've ever given myself. Just allowing myself to go back to the childhood state, through a child like state of just observing and taking things at face value. It's not been easy. I went from a pattern of controlling and then this gradually dropped away. However, the old religious training from being a preacher's child came up that I needed to save people. So being loving, translated from being and using my word as my bond, to now I needed to save people. I went through many years of that, actually trying to save people, giving them my opinions about how they should live their lives.

Then I realized that that was creating a huge set of stresses, a whole bunch of connections to people that really didn't want to change which is fine cause that's their journey. I had to let it all go completely. I almost stopped this journey. I almost stopped working with technologies of embodiment, technologies of enlightenment. I almost stopped the whole thing, but what kept me going was Ann, The Team, the Team of beings who love me without condition. They don't put pressure on me they just accept me. I realize that saving others is not about loving myself - that is my ego. My doing service to mankind is not loving. It is about pacifying my ego's feeling of not being in alignment with my journey.

Surrendering into a state of love is the biggest gift you can give yourself. It is not easy. You can go take a whole bunch of courses on it, search the world, spend $1 million dollars, you can dance the dance, but until you realize that the only way to surrender is through self-love, you will find delusional feelings of surrender projected from your ego. When you truly let go and love, you will understand you know nothing. This is what I had to do. So why should I impose my beliefs on another's journey of abuse, or their journey of love, their journey of radical change or their journey of repeating the same dysfunctional relationship attachments? It's their journey. It's not mine. I just need to love myself, love them, and hold space where they can feel that they are safe. I encourage you to do the same.

Love yourself. Honour yourself. Surrender not to the ego but to the soul that you are! It is through this that we all participate in creating and bringing into reality a change and shift - a hope for humanity.

CLOSING REMARKS

So, you, the reader, have read this far. Potentially, you have been challenged to think that there might be real change taking place in your world. You may even begin to sense the spark of hope for this place you live in, this world. Some of you are oscillating in this moment between hope and despair, hope and despair, and that is okay. But through these words that have been given to you, whether they are the galactic language or the English language, the intention is merely to inspire you to take action by awakening and surrendering to love, self-love.

Taking action does not mean that you have to go running out in the street, phone everybody, or send out a million emails. For each of you, taking action is something very different. For some of you taking action, it'll merely be in practicing surrender. That is taking an intention of moving to surrendering through love and bringing it into a reality within you. Others that are at states of surrender already, we remind you, that without love in your life, without this embodiment of neutrality and acceptance of each and every being and thing on your planet, you truly only make minor change.

As you observe thoughts and ideas, the next step is to choose and take action. In taking action, let go of the outcomes. Some of you are very action-oriented. You have been running around doing many things without focus, and that is fine. You're merely creating many, many, many expansion opportunities for you. Now, if you choose to change that pattern, just let go of the outcomes. Trust and surrender the outcome, go into a state of love and then, when needed and when inspired, take action again.

So, this message may seem to be a repeat of what we've said, but it is clear that we want to see you understand the value of surrendering to love of all things beautiful in your life. We repeat - all things of love and beauty in your life are a result of the vibration of love. We will not go into the negative side. It is not relevant to this communication. So, remember, if you want and desire love, joy and, peace, then let go, surrender, and then take action with your life.

We have been honoured to be part of this communication to you. We are connected to you, not separate from you. Many of you reading this book contributed to these pieces of communication. So, if it feels true to you, then it is a truth. Be at peace.

ANN AND BILL'S STORY

So, who are Ann, Bill and the Team we refer to? Not sure ourselves some days, but let's gives this a go....

Ann and Bill have been together for many, many lives and in many, many universes playing with and understanding the human potential through love. It is why they came together in love at this time, in this space. In this union of two beings, they have dedicated their lives to each other's expansion and evolution through love. What do you choose?

Who is the Team we refer to in this book? It's a collective of ancient beings of which we are a part of, dedicated to non-interference and expansion through love in the universe(s). In this book we tried to separate Ann, Bill, and The Team. We are strongly reminded even as we write this that we are all in this together, hence the word Team, Team Love.

Come meet Ann, Bill, and Team Love by going to www.MeetAnnandBill.ca.

As part of the completion of this book, Ann, Bill and others have been inspired to provide hope in their own way, through love. For more details on how you might participate in a change through love, go to https://loveevolution.ca/hope-4-humanity-inititiatives/

Ann and Bill

CHAPTER 5

RETURN TO LOVE THROUGH AWARENESS AND FAITH

Faith

Prime Creator aka Spirit aka Big Kahuna
Transcribed by Anna Trillana

To come back to unity, you must first be separated from it; to come back to love, you must first be engulfed in fear; to connect empathetically and learn compassion, you must first experience suffering.

To know thyself, you must first un-know yourself then proceed through the journey to reconnect back to your true self. To appreciate the stars at night, you need the darkness to allow them to shine through. To learn from your wounds and heal them, the wound must be exposed and triggered. You live in the enterprise of dichotomy - its structures define the Earthly dimension you are in.

The collaborators of this book and their work were brought together to co-create unique frequencies to resonate with the many unique individuals on this planet. Each individual in this book channels the same message of awareness, love, hope, and oneness through their own unique experiences, understandings, and connections to Spirit.

Anna's message this time is not about sharing her current life journey. She was asked to provide a sliver of it in the previous book in which she uncomfortably participated; and she has now again.

Each individual's process of channeling or transcribing information is unique and beautiful. Anna channels information every moment, daily for others as a psychotherapist, energy practitioner, teacher, and author. This gets her out of her own comfort zone to become more vulnerable with others by providing the messages wc have asked her to share, with the flare that she brings.

One of Anna's purposes is to reach out to individuals by sharing the challenges she continues to overcome as an opportunity to teach others how to heal themselves. Her vulnerability provides the opportunity to connect with others and bring awareness, trust, compassion, empathy and understanding in her work. Ultimately, she is a true conduit of compassion, humility, and unconditional love.

Anna continues to fight the discomfort of being private and introverted. She works with us to expose herself by publicly modeling being comfortable with the uncomfortable. Only then can one truly heal, progress and evolve. This is the co-creation of the ultimate good and highest benefit of all. Even as we say this about her, she uncomfortably shies away, not wanting to be put on the spot or given acclamation for the progress made in her many lifetimes here on Earth.

We are all spirits; aspects who are connected to our prime creator, Spirit. During her interactions with others, some of **Us** involve her clients', students', loved ones' and her own guidance committees. However, the majority of her collaboration is with **Me, the Big Kahuna**, as she likes to call **Me, Prime Creator** aka **Spirit**. It is amusing to watch Anna when my other name, God, comes up despite her understanding that I am all those. I AM. I am one with her and I am one with all of you. You have given me many names throughout the timelines and sometimes this noun produces a negative stigma, residue, or vibration from others' experiences throughout their lifetimes. She feels this discordance of vibration that has imposed others to experience separation from the truth, from love, from oneness. Nonetheless, I am the oneness and the love that always remains, despite the many shadows of fear that reside on your planet and in your minds.

With the introductions out of the way, the need for her to step back in and provide the messages by me about Unity is necessary more so now than ever. No longer are competition and separation required. It is merely feedback from one's experience that needs realignment. However, awareness is the key to the change. To heal, to be, to love oneself completely. In turn, to be one with me. To return to love. The shadows of the ego are necessary for your learning and it has kept my love volume down for you, causing you to feel separated from me and your true selves. Exposing such shadows of the ego is what provides a different perspective and the miracles towards your freedom.

Themes will be provided for your understanding. See this as a new user manual in your awakening to the awareness of life around you. Purposely, none of you came with a manual on how to properly cope with your feelings, or how to behave, or communicate with others, or how to be a parent, or how to be in a relationship. This was all divinely orchestrated to create the lessons and the processes to unlearn your past programs that you all have downloaded into this lifetime, in order to appreciate and unravel your true self and return back to love, to me.

There is not one way nor one right or wrong path in discovering the truth of who you really are. You are more than just the body you are in. You are more than the just the role you play at work or at home. You are more than just the experiences you have gained. You are all divine spiritual beings having a human experience in a human physical body.

Just like there are many unique frequencies upon the planet and unique individuals; there too, are many paths towards enlightenment that have many interpretations of wisdom and peace. Truly, when you have said, "I see the light," it is to denote understanding. Light carries information and information can be challenging to accept.

Just as enlightenment may not be as pleasant as others expect during their discoveries. Enlightenment is sitting in the middle and understanding the importance of both pain and peace; the yin and the yang. (Don't worry we will get into that later). For now, the realization is that there is no right or wrong, nor one ultimate way towards your path to freedom and love. Therefore, you cannot choose what is best for each person. You can only choose for yourself. Here lies the dismissal of judgment, separation and the illusion of competition. This we will also get into more deeply later.

Language alone cannot provide full understanding. It is

through your experiences and processes that you truly gain further deeper awareness, and ultimate evolution.

Reading a book, taking a class, obtaining knowledge and insight, are only fragments of the process required to change a behaviour. If one is trying to stop smoking, drinking or eating unhealthy foods, the required steps are rarely sufficient to implement the systematic changes necessary for the desired outcome to manifest. Deeper understanding and awareness of the root causes for such behaviours are essential in order to take appropriate actions when triggers occur. This allows access to recreate a different response that one seeks to change. Being more consistently mindful with your actions and acknowledging they are equally intertwined with your emotional and spiritual bodies grounds the new system for the desired behaviour, lifestyle, and mindset. Being more present, grounded and unified with all there is provides the key to dismissing the autopilot or survival mode that has caused you all to forget who you truly are - the unlimited capacity to love, and the unlimited potential to be more than your fears.

Change cannot come without specific, repetitive actions and specific, mindful intentions. Just like your many lifetimes you choose to come back to reapply new lessons for evolution, everything is a mirroring effect, as above, so below, in heaven as is on earth. All dilemmas and thought patterns are mimicked throughout every event repeating itself over and over until it is fully grounded and realized. Awareness provides you the gateway to your freedom and your future self. Remember, Carl Jung says, "I am not what happened to me. I am who I choose to become." You can learn what has happened to you and why you are where you are today. Once insight has been achieved, you can choose again and again to co-create a new way of being, a new way of living, and a new way towards love simply by looking at a different perspective. This optimizes your mindset and acquires the necessary integration of mind, body and spirit.

PROCESS OF A SOUL HAVING A HUMAN EXPERIENCE

Many of you have come across different materials and understanding of the complexities of soul incarnations. Many of the collaborators will touch upon them as well. There is not just one way of understanding any subject, matter or action; the human language alone doesn't give justice to the complete depth of knowledge required to understand your soul's processes. There are some beings on this planet and even in this book who have high comprehension in understanding the entirety of the soul and universal processes. This is solely based on their own souls' education and their roles outside of the human body. Yes, you can have many alternative lives at the same time as you are manifested as this human now.

Analogies are very beautiful and beneficial for human conceptualization. Imagine you are an assistant to the chief doctor on the Starship Enterprise like in Star Trek, and you ask your superior if and when would you be able to become the lead doctor of your own ship. They review your progress records (Akashic records) along with the criteria required to take on such responsibility. Your Akashic records indicate that there is a self-punishment program that is at 75% and the job in question requires the value to be at 10%. Therefore, your superiors say that in order to bring that value of self-punishment down, you require further training. The training would provide the opportunity to work on self-punishment by contracting you in self-punishing events. How you handle and overcome these self-punishing events will either decrease or increase the self-punishment percentage. If you continue to decrease the value, you will advance in your role to become the lead doctor of your own ship.

Let's take this into a deeper level. You have all asked me to provide you patience. Yet, I have done so by providing you impatient events for you to learn to choose patience. You can only gain required energy by creating or recreating it yourselves in the opportune environments that support its presence. In order to heal self-punishment, you need to be in the environment where self-punishment exists, exposing you to the opportunity to choose not to punish yourself. You can only heal wounds when they are being exposed or being triggered.

The training field is done in a holographic room and here you co-create all the required elements for your learning. You choose all the sufficient parameters and designs including specific people, events and challenges which will provide you the opportunity to learn and decrease the self-punishment program. All alternative paths from A – Z are selected including the moment when you are at a fork in the road. You have alternative paths from A-Z to select from. Whatever road you chose from A-Z is pre-set with its own challenges and opportunities.

Each A-Z route not only includes specific events, it also include specific partners, family members, coworkers, friends, foes, and even strangers to push your buttons to help you be exposed to self-punishment programs. These were all pre-set and chosen by you, the individuals involved in the pre-set events, and your team. It is complex as indicated.

Once all the pre-sets are chosen, they are then reviewed and evaluated to see if you acquire the sufficient skills found in your Akashic records to overcome the routes outlined on your chosen journey. If they are out of your scope, some plans are removed from your design.

You are supported with a team during your entire life training process. They provide guidance without interfering in your choices. All of these pre-sets and information are then temporarily wiped from your memory, only accessible to you when it is pre-set to turn back on. Some are not meant to have this pre-set feature turned on; this is why you may see others not taking on the roles to become aware. This is also why there are some that are pre-set earlier in their lives to remember who they are, how the universe works, and how to be more in tune with their surroundings. This, too, is a pre-set feature.

Thus, the beliefs, perceptions, and judgments on others' life experiences versus their age is very distorted. Not every 60-year-old is as tuned-in or experienced as a 10-year-old and vice versa. You are not meant to know what each individual has contracted to take on in his or her journeys, nor do you know how evolved and old their souls are. The majority of the time they are not pre-set to know themselves. Superficial external features are only part of holographic illusion.

The Big Kahuna is the last reviewer and ultimate decision maker by placing their stamp of approval on it. "Okay, you can handle this. Good luck on your journey. I am always with you even when you purposely forget."

Purposely forgetting occurs when all of your memories of the holographic training set-up and plans are temporarily removed, until the pre-set is chosen to turn back either during your journey in the hologram or when you have completed the journey.

This holographic arena is your Earth. The role you are currently playing is the training parameters set for you to gain more experience to decrease the self-punishment down to 10% instead of 75%. Once this holographic game/lifetime is over, you are not judged or criticized for your experiences, but you are encouraged to understand the choices you made and what they provided for your evolution. The choices upon Earth may require further training if specific goals have not been achieved to become the lead doctor on a ship, as the example provided. The goals differ from becoming a guide, a guardian angel, an etheric surgeon, a committee member, to another person while they are incarnated on Earth.

This is only a fragment of the incarnation process. You may say, "I choose all my experiences??? Why would I choose this? What was I thinking?" The answer is yes and no. It was chosen both by you, by all the agreed players in the chosen life experience, your support team, and ultimately the final say comes from me, Spirit, aka Big Kahuna, aka Prime Creator, aka I AM, aka Source...you get it... You are fully supported, guided, and loved. Each experience provides a beautiful learning lesson, which is why there is no such thing as a mistake or a failed action. They produce much gain in your life development, despite the painful perceptions they can hold. Again, we will discuss this further later in this transcription.

It must be highlighted that not one person is less or more than the other. If this were so, it would indicate there is judgment on each being. This is not the case. An innocent, pure being of love has no judgment against them, for there is nothing to judge an innocent, and you all are pure innocent souls who are loved beyond all measure. Each unique being plays many different roles and different experiences, but again that does not mean that any individual is favored amongst the rest.

Each employee is just as important as the role of the employee who manages and oversees them; every employee plays a vital part in the intricacies of the universal processes.

Yes, there are many who achieve further development that have been popularized on your Earth, but they too have their own Akashic Records, challenges, continual evolution, and requirements to fulfill. Such beings may choose to return to Earth only to serve and help without the purpose of further training, but still have to abide by the rules and regulations of the planet they return to. This means they would have to incarnate, and still feel and have human emotional challenges and triggers around them. No one is exempt from the rules, as no one has favoritism from Spirit. Therefore, even though such beings may have achieved enlightenment, it does not mean they get a "Get Out of Jail Free Card" or a "Pass Go and collect $200" card.

Each planet has its own set rules and requirements that all must experience, despite their skillset, mastery or enlightenment. Earth is the planet of emotion. All those who inhabit Earth must adhere to the frequencies of learning through the emotional strains and challenges that the Earth provides. All beings must go through specific roles, outcomes and experiences, as any would. Therefore, you may not even realize who is amongst you: Jesus, Buddha, St. Germaine, Mary, Kwan Yin, to name a few, have all lived amongst you without your awareness of who they truly are. Some are even still here now, fully aware of their true spiritual essence whilst playing the current human role they are in and still feeling, learning, and overcoming the challenges of this lifetime. This is why there is no need to judge your brothers or sisters. If you truly knew their essence, you would treat them differently, with high esteem and respect. However, this again would denote favoritism and dismissing the experience to accept everyone as equal and one with all. Remember that song, "What if God was one of us? Just a stranger on the bus?" The validity of this song is another avenue, or sign, as you call it, towards discovering the truth for who you are and the remembering to return to love.

To this end, you are ALL loved, you are ALL special, and you are ALL needed as you are NOW with ALL of the aspects you are contributing in.

There is no benefit or purpose for anyone to know what you are here to learn or vice versa. As you start to wake up and learn about the freedom that exists right in front of you, it doesn't mean you have the right to interfere in others' processes or paths towards their awakening by taking on and uncovering their work for them. They need to discover it for themselves. You would be robbing them of their experiences and process in learning where they need to go and how, or when. It is understandable that it is difficult to witness your loved ones suffer, so to speak, when you can see the potential and beauty around them as you have witnessed from your own lessons; but again, not everyone is meant to change, gain awareness, or wake up. Therefore, judgment of others is not only discordant to your soul and theirs, but also collectively to all.

Why would anyone choose to not wake up when there is much beauty, freedom and peace to be gained? Quite simply it is because they are not meant to wake up in this lifetime. As indicated above, some are meant to just push your buttons, causing you to choose to react or not, participating in your perception and providing an opportunity for you to learn. This can be overwhelming and confusing. That is why it is called a process that is to be digested in layers over time. If you were to become aware of the complete complexity of your own life and how the universe works, your human brain would not be able to handle it. It would be like a computer short-circuiting from too much information when it doesn't have proper supportive components to function.

As you unlock layers in your learning processes, supportive components are provided so you may handle new information and lessons. However, these are gained from repetitive programming so that is engrained into your memory circuits. Whenever you ask, "Why is this happening TO me?" Really, it is happening FOR you. For your learning, you have chosen your capacity which can be handled at the timeframe pre-set for you.

Understanding this criterion will allow you to start moving into the perspective of forgiveness. When you acknowledge that you all have chosen to play this video game with one another, you can accept that all relationships are necessary even when they are not always pleasant. You are all playing roles. That doesn't mean that what is experienced on Earth is acceptable, or right, or wrong. Please look at it as if from the aspect of the eyes of a director, shooting a movie, observing all the pieces to the story and changing it as needed. Every actor plays a fictional part, far from who they truly are which is divine spiritual beings, innocent and pure. When we are absorbed in the movie we are acting in, we get lost in the story believing that it is real because it feels real. We forget that we've elected to participate in the perception for a reason. In that moment we are not aware of being on the holographic set called Earth.

UNDERSTANDING THE HUMAN BEHAVIOUR
SURVIVAL MODE = FEAR

Any pain originates from beliefs, perceptions, and expectations from your past experience. These beliefs, perceptions, and judgments have blocked you from seeing love, being empathetic, compassionate, patient, and forgiving to people and events you are involved in. Wounds that are imprinted upon you at a young age are necessary and inevitable means for your learning journey.

You would not become the person you are without the experiences you've had. Without suffering, you would not have the opportunity to understand compassion.

Without impatient situations, you would not have the opportunity to learn patience. Your wounds paint or taint your perceptions in your day-to-day lives, causing unique reactions imposing fear and ridicule to yourself or towards others, both consciously and unconsciously. The wounds imprint on everyone and some can be louder or more painful than others. These wounds include rejection, neglect, abandonment, abuse, loss, betrayal and guilt. They repeat throughout your lifetime, and if left unaddressed, unacknowledged, and inappropriately managed will continue to create the illusion of suffering.

This illusion of suffering creates the impression that you are being punished for choices you have made in current or previous lifetimes. I say this to you: I could not punish those who I love, just as you would not punish an innocent lamb and condemn it to suffering and misery. You are not judged by me, but by the shadows of your thoughts and perceptions narrating through your minds. You forget that you are loved, whole, and accepted no matter what you do or don't do. I love you. Your actions are but pivotal roles from pre-sets and opportunities you co-created to affect the situations you are in. They provide alternative routes and choices towards love or cyclical programming of fear. Your team of shadows or your ego's aspects are devised to manipulate your thoughts causing you to feel discordant emotions, which would cause you to choose behaviours to avoid the reopening the wounds.

The Shadows have many names from different approaches and books provided from me to others. In one perspective they are known as the Critic, Incompetent, Politician, Martyr, Paranoid, Rebel, and Royal. They create dialogue in your mind tricking you to believe that they are your thoughts and creating notions to push you to behave a certain way to complete their vicious cycle of debilitating behaviours.

Essentially, the Shadows believe they are doing their best to protect you by going into a fight, flight, or freeze behaviour mode. Your team of shadows manipulate your thoughts at your expense, in a very damaging and distorted way, to enhance the addictive pattern towards survival and comfort. These patterns of comfort and survival can involve a variety of distractions, avoidance, and combative tactics to diffuse the discomfort of the triggered wounds. These patterns can be both healthy and unhealthy coping behaviours that can become debilitating to one's evolution. Familiar, immediate gratification patterns to diffuse triggered wounds occur when we feel sad, fearful, angry, deprived, stressed, or bored. They appear in ways which can include: FLIGHT: working too much, taking on much more than necessary, engaging in drugs and alcohol, eating or not eating, sex, travelling, shopping, fixing others instead of fixing yourself, being codependent on others to fill your loneliness.
FREEZE: isolating and shutting down, avoiding others.
FIGHT: starting conflicts and fights, blaming others, and more.

All of these fight, flight and freeze behaviours are tempted by your Shadows. These survival behaviours are used to distract and fill the void, instead of acknowledging your feelings and appropriately doing the work to heal. They are programmed and automatically set to override anything else that would be more appropriate for your growth and healing, thus creating the addictive process to numb oneself or justify their behaviours due to the pains they have experienced. Any healthy behaviour can be easily manipulated inappropriately, thus diverting you into immediate gratification to gain comfort at all costs, causing painful outcomes with others and with your healing and growth. This act not only prevents you from healing and growing, it also derails your path to return to love.

Rejection wound example: James, a 9-year-old child waits to get picked on a team to play dodge ball. Sarah and Mark lead the selection process, both publicly humiliating James and refusing to select him for their teams. This loud and painful message of disdain imprints upon James that he is not good enough and that no one accepts him or wants him. From the critical comments the Ego Shadow, Critic, emerges.

This Critic speaks the same dismissive, poisonous and rejecting language that the children made and James carries the thoughts into his adult years that he will never be accepted or enough unless he engages in specific coping behaviours to either gain acceptance or avoid rejection from others. Enter the flight coping survival behaviour which can involve James drinking his stresses away in order for him to feel comfortable despite the fact these actions enhance further harm. Thus, the seemingly protective Critic shadow is only a discordant coping mechanism that doesn't heal the rejection wound. Instead it persists in James' life as limitation, misery, and fear.

What you are not aware of, you cannot change. You must first understand what you are doing or not doing, where it resides, and when the trigger occurs. This allows you to create an action before the vicious cycle begins.

Awareness is key to change. How you think creates how you feel, and in turn, how you behave. What you think persists. (The Law of Attraction) If you choose to keep thinking you are doomed and unworthy, all your experiences will highlight only doom and defeat. Where there is loss, there is also gain. In the same perception, if you choose to realign your focus, you will see that there is light amidst the darkness with opportunities and great blessings. Where there is pain, there is peace. Pain and struggle are constant as the parameters on Earth for your learning, but there is also peace that is constant as well, should you choose to access it. Therefore, there are inevitable, continuous storms lined up ready and waiting for you once the current storm clears. Every single moment is but a preparation for the next storm, and all the future storms that are pre-set to come. These storms are pre-set to activate the wounds you have chosen to work on in this lifetime. The shadows can be used against you or for you, either wreaking havoc in your mind engaging in destructive behaviours, or they can be used as signals for you to realign yourself by challenging their damnations against you.

SUPPORT & SIGNS

Your guidance teams work with you to help you to find your way back from fear to love. You may have seen them when you find dimes, feathers, repeating numbers,

phrases from others, gut feelings and more. These are not coincidences. Really, I say to you that there are no such things as coincidences, only pre-set moments in your time to remember who you are which is a divine spiritual being participating as a human on Earth with the parameters of yin and yang, pain and peace.

Remember the story involving a man waiting to be rescued from a flood. This man, we will call Joe, refuses to evacuate his home; telling his neighbours to go on without him because "My God will save me". The flood rises forcing him to go to the second floor of his home when a policeman on a boat comes by the window offering him to get into the boat to save him. Refusing the second time, he states, "My God will save me." As the flood rises further, Joe waits on his rooftop and when a helicopter pilot sends down the ladder to get him to safety, he motions his refusal because "My God will save me." The flood inevitably engulfs Joe, who asks, "God why didn't you save me?" To which I replied, "I did. I sent your neighbours, the police, and helicopter pilot to save you and you refused every time. I have always been there, but your perception prevented you from continuing the life you were living".

You are not as alone as you may feel physically. You are supported and loved and continuously given guidance. It is but your ability to sense it and trust it to know its truth. Faith in this is strengthened with your constant awareness. Practice in acquiring the lessons you learn, because as previously indicated, they will unlock more of your memory of who you are and why you chose to be here. They also unlock your intuition and the gifts that ALL of you have from the beginning of time. Once again, some of you have pre-sets that allow you to utilize them on this journey and some of you have not. As you gain more and more awareness, every choice, every thought you think, every feeling you have is connected to everything.

You all have been guided towards many avenues to self-realization. One size does not fit all. You are all unique, vibrating at your own unique frequencies constantly shifting to your own tune and in your own time. This is why there has been an influx of teachers, authors, speakers, religions, modalities, books, tools and loved ones. All the answers have always been within you and you have many resources within your reach. The difficulty is the doing what you already know and hear thousands of times to get you back to love. Yet, the ability to do so has been masked by the temptations of the shadows to engage in comforting, yet debilitating, behaviours. To heal and grow you must be comfortable with all of your discomforts and limitations to break through the fear and return to love.

BOUNDARIES: THE DISTANCE BETWEEN OTHERS AND YOUR FEARS

As perception shifts, ownership and accountability shift as you come into acceptance that every reaction is a projection of one's fears and wounds. If someone imposes his or her judgment on to you, this transference is a reflection of their fears within him or her. It may be that the judge lacks something that the person being judged possesses, or perhaps both the judge and the person being judged have a common quality, and the judge does not want to acknowledge that quality.

If one judges another for the appearance of being selfish, it is only a reflection that the judge lacks in self-love for themself. Everyone is using each other as a punching bag, inflicting their pain on others both unconsciously and consciously. Be accountable for your reactions that they are feedback to your system that your wound has been triggered. You would not have reacted if there were no wounds to trigger. Therefore, anyone inflicting judgment is only a reflection of them imposing their wounds onto you. It is not a personal attack because you can never be attacked unless you believe you are, and you need to defend. But I say this, there is nothing to defend because there is truly nothing to attack. Love cannot be attacked and love does not need to defend.

Freedom lies in your perception; you can choose to believe you are being attacked and focus on the loss from it, or you can choose to see the truth that it has nothing to do with you. The person seemingly attacking you is trying to release their wounds and pain on to you too, so that your reaction will soothe their pain and avoid them from self-regulation and ownership. If you choose to redirect the focus of your reactions to those who are only of your own accord and control, their reactions, perceptions, and judgments are theirs, not yours; you gain peace and freedom.

No one can do the work for you but you. Also, no one can make you see what you are not ready to see or incapable of seeing. If you choose to take on the role of doing the work for others and limit their ability to take ownership, as previously discussed, you are interfering in their journey. Meddling in others' paths is a boundary issue. You believe you know what is best for them. Providing unsolicited direction or information is another act of fear. Loving support involves listening, providing space for one to feel safe to unravel their struggles to you, and asking them what you can do for them; not imposing what you feel is best for them but redirecting them to professionals they can employ to help guide them to hear their truth and options within them. Taking on others' pain is not for you to take on if you are not skilled with the appropriate measures to protect both your own energetic boundaries and theirs.

Upon your awakening, you may feel you can decipher someone else's journey because you have unlocked your own. I say to you this, do not be so quick to judge that the perceived losses that your wounds and shadows focus you to see is the same loss that is happening for them. Remember, what you see is unique to you, because you have your own past and pre-set options, just as they do. Alternatively, the one you see as imbalanced with your perception of loss may actually not be imbalanced, but purposely assigned to share insight through the perceived disadvantaged experience by showing others how they overcame the shadows and healed themselves by focusing on blessed gain from the blessed loss.

BOUNDARY OF SELF WORTH

Your self-worth is not gained by devaluing yourself or your experience. Everything in your world is energy and everything is the process of energy exchange. (The Law of Cause and Effect). If you choose to constantly devalue the work you do and give it away for free, you are meddling and interfering with the receiver's ability to take accountability by exchanging their energy with you. I have said many times that I AM with YOU. We are one and if you do not value yourself then you do not value me. I do not see less of you so why do you see less of yourself? Energy exchange equals healthy boundaries, which are vital, because without them the parties involved will be at a disadvantage in their learning, healing and evolutionary process.

To perceive that one must martyr and sacrifice themselves so that it validates their worthiness is but the act of the shadow that is enforcing self-destruction by giving your work for free or apologizing for wrongs that you are not responsible for. Avoid doing work for others you are not responsible to take on and avoid breaking your boundaries by walking away or saying no instead of yes. Breaking boundaries opens layers to your fields that creates imbalance to yourself and to the other person involved, again impacting each other's processes and evolution. This is FLIGHT behaviour, a discordant coping mechanism activated to prevent wounds from reopening.

Providing a perceived selfless gesture is an illusion that the shadow imposes for you to see that by breaking such boundaries you are interfering in other's process for your selfish gain - to gain validation that you are a good person. It has been said many times, you already ARE a good person, and any distorted beliefs, perceptions or behaviours you think you need to act upon are only fear. How is sacrificing and depriving oneself an act of love? Unconditional love does not make illusionary demands on the innocent. Conditions and demands would not equate to unconditional love, but fear. You are worthy to say no; you are worthy enough to just be. You are more than enough to also accept energy exchange, just as the other person involved is worthy to give the energy exchange for their own purposes.

MOVING FROM FEAR TO LOVE

Every moment of your journey provides you the opportunity to gain the skillset to manage and recognize fear by redirecting your thoughts, actions, and feelings towards love. Every choice you make creates experiences to increase or decrease your vibrations, resonating with your environment, grounding you into love or paralyzing you into fear. Each choice you make is based on your perceptions and feelings from past experiences. You are not usually upset about what you think you are upset about. It is in the how that is important for your healing including how you choose the actions you choose to take, how you choose to think, and how you choose to see and feel.

It is inevitable to have painful challenges, as this is the constant playground for you to adapt towards choosing the opportunities of peace.

The Law of Cause and Effect has been highlighted throughout this transcription. How you care for your mind, your body, and your soul is vital to moving from fear to love. This in turn affects your world as a collective. You do not need to be a healer or practitioner to create a change in the world. You have heard Gandhi tell you, "Be the change you want to see in the world." You are rippling effects with one another because everything is connected to everything. Everything comes back to oneness with Me. The impact of this chain reaction effect can be seen when a traffic officer stands in the middle of the busiest highway controlling the flow of the drivers' ability to get to and fro on their journeys.

You cannot expect to gain higher frequencies and access more knowledge or abilities when the actions that are chosen decrease your frequencies with discordant thoughts, feelings or actions. Think about the actions you choose to engage in. What are the intentions behind them? What are they filling? Is there a justification that you can and will, and it won't cause an effect because you are human, and you deserve to have the drink of wine or piece of cake or...? These are all fueled by fear, not love. If you return to love, you know there is no need to do anything but to be. Be present to fill yourself with love by connecting and grounding within yourself and accessing your unlimited potential.

YOUR PURPOSE = BE-ING

Hope is the acknowledgment that everything has the ability to change for the better. It is the awareness that is based on how we choose to think, behave and feel, inevitably creating a different outcome not only for your own personal world, but also for everyone around you and the planet you live on.

Forgive yourself for the truth, enlightening your field. Forgive yourself for the path and perceptions you realize you have chosen to know thus far. Forgive others for participating in your perception of the movie that you are in.

Forgiveness does not mean that what has been done is dismissed or allowed. It is the promise to release you from your painful and limiting experiences and from being the victim in your pre-set perceptions. Release the fear that shadows hold on you and allow love to free you of the poison enabling compassion with yourself and others involved. Know that everyone is doing the best that they can with the capacity they are at. You are all perfectly imperfect humans. Everyone is playing a part for you to gain experience, healing, and growth. No one received the manual of life to show them how to cope appropriately, how to understand themselves and their behaviours, or how to be a parent, a friend or a lover to others.

The purpose of being on Earth is be-ing. Your purpose is to move from fear to love and be happy be-ing. The truth is revealed as you grow and unlock the different levels of your videogame. Everything is happening FOR you and not TO you. You are NOT a helpless victim. You are the co-creator in your purposeful life. See that nothing is defective, incompetent or hopeless, because that alone is living in fear and void of the truth. Everything has its purpose to provide the lesson it needs. Remember the dichotomy: your existence serves purpose only till its existence is no longer purposeful. This is when you have achieved the realization that everything is one.

You and everyone else are not lacking anything. You are always, have been, and already are enough. You are whole. Your choices create the changes to your world, to your humanity. Be mindful for the highest good and highest purpose for all.

Everything from what you drink to what you eat affects your feelings, thoughts, abilities and most importantly, it affects your Earth and everyone around you. It is the

Law of Cause and Effect. The plastic you choose to bag your fruits and vegetables creates a chain reaction in your world. The choice of food such as the meat you eat and how much you consume of it creates an impact in the world's pollution. The choice to create more conveniences and comforts creates impact to the world. Everything is connected to everything. When you move from Fear to Love, you are more in tune and connected to everything. You are mindful with love to choose behaviours that can create a beneficial chain reaction for you, others, and the world you are in.

Trust that all things are working well for you and are divinely orchestrated. They are divinely timed according to the blueprint of your life, experienced as a soul in this world, as a human.

You all have the answers within you and everything you need to be free. You have been provided with all the avenues you need for your journey to be filled with grace, love and joy. It is all in your own choosing. You are not lacking anything. It is only the perception you choose to hold that creates this distorted belief. Find your joy and if you need to change your path to continue to follow your joy, then do so. However, know this, you do not have to impress me, or anyone. You don't have to do anything or not do anything. Just Be.

I love you and I am always with you; you need but only call and you need only to learn to listen and see.

Anna's Story

Anna's purpose is teaching others compassion and acceptance with integrity, guiding them with their daily demands and personal crises. As a therapist, healer, teacher and author, she challenges individuals to face their discomforts, triggers and wounds in an unconditionally loving and nonjudgmental way. Anna believes everyone is on their own unique journey in discovering their truth and the potential to become unlimited.

Anna continues to openly share her previous and current struggles with her clients to help inspire, relate, and motivate them that they are not alone, and they are truly understood. Her vulnerability and encouragement with others trail blazes new routes for humanity in recognizing there is always another way, another perspective to heal ourselves no matter how challenging our journeys can be. A sliver of her life story is shared in another collaboration, Amazon's #1 Best Seller, *The Beauty of Authenticity,* where she tells the story of how she viewed her life path and shows what she did with the experiences. She now uses her own story to lead others to find hope in their own struggles, and to show them that there is proof anything is possible when we surrender our judgments, perceptions and beliefs to allow ourselves to live a life of love instead of fear. The true access of hope is to have faith and trust in the process that we can choose again and create another alternative to our experiences.

With her fiancé, Andrew, they customize their clients'

needs at their Mind, Body and Soul center, Infinite Strength, both in person in Fort McMurray, Alberta and online worldwide. Distance is of no bounds for these two in guiding others to their unlimited potential. Andrew's expertise as a humorous and understanding Movement & Nutrition Specialist (background in Kinesiology, Functional Movement, Chiropractic, Nutrition, and Personal Coaching & Development) grounds Anna's evolving integration of Psychotherapy, Hypnotherapy, Embodied work (Reiki, IET, SRT, Qi Gong, Ayurveda, & Yoga), Sound Therapy, and more.

Anna continues to work with Spirit every moment of her day with students and clients providing many opportunities in grounding their mind, body and spirit through the guidance of Spirit.

Together, Andrew and Anna's experiences, training and intuitive abilities guide their clients to become comfortable with being uncomfortable in order for them to evolve and heal. They are dedicated in promoting understanding and healing with one's past and present to change their futures by instilling seeds of self-awareness, self-care, and self-love to groups, individuals, and couples of all ages and all locations.

Anna Trillana

Website: www.infinitestrength.ca
Email: info@infinitestrength.ca
Facebook: www.facebook.com/infinitestrength.ca/
Instagram: @infinitestrength.ca

CHAPTER 6

RETURN TO ONENESS

Surrender

by Arianna Zimmer

*I allow myself to be the clear and perfect channel that
I am, allowing energies, messages of the highest
vibrational capacity and those most assisting at this
time, to flow fluidly, clearly, easily, and completely into this
time, into this now, serving Humanity, all that choose, in the
highest capacity, now.*

*With that, I ask to begin, and in channeling my questions
for all those that are here in love and support and serving, I
ask the following questions:*

HOW DO WE SHED WHAT IT IS THAT WE THINK WE ARE, AND ALLOW OURSELVES TO MOVE INTO WHAT IT IS THAT WE TRULY ARE? THANK YOU.

I would love to answer this question at this time. And by
the way, it is a beautiful question. Thank you for asking it
in such a sweet and complete and careful and caring way.
This question will be answered uniquely and differently
for every individual who chooses to receive the answer to

this question, making it their own. But we would like to give a more overall, holistic answer for all the minds and beings who choose this.

Each of us has learned over our own evolution, for lack of a better word, over and across our own journey, what it is like to move into and out of higher vibrating frequencies. Some of this is done in a more linear fashion, as humanity is experiencing, to some extent. Some of us have learned this by moving through what you would call timelines, or energy portals, or dimensions, or lives. But we have experienced it in a nonlinear or non-chronological fashion. That being said, we have experienced, many of us have experienced these same transitional experiences, same transitional qualities, that you are experiencing now. We have experienced that growth, that answer to the calling of moving into a higher echelon, higher vibration, higher growth capacity. We feel this in all of your hearts now: the answering, the highest answering of the current calling that you are being called to now.

As easy as it is to say (and maybe harder to do), let go of the mind chatter. Let go of all the pre-dispositioned beliefs, understandings, wants, hopes, desires - for those are all learned through an already predetermined vantage or point of view. You learned through an experiential formula what it was like to be human when born into many of the societies that we are communicating with now. As we let go of more and more of these ideas and beliefs, and it's all happening now, there will be a clearer vantage that can be seen from, where the I is released into the greater I, the I AM, the Wholeness, the Oneness.

We would like to paint for you a metaphorical picture.

So many of us come with marks on our canvas. We have placed them there ourselves; our societies have placed them there unbeknownst to us; unconsciously. That is okay. That is what has been experienced until now. And now that higher calling, that higher vibration, is asking, not for you to paint over what is there, but to allow the canvas itself to let go of the markings, to let go of the pigment that has adhered to its surface, so that it just floats off of the canvas.

And again, one returns to a child-like, unknown, open, wondering space of receiving and receivership. No thing needs to be defended, honoured, clung-to, held, nothing; for it has been released from the canvas and nothing is asked to be added new to this canvas, but to look at the canvas and honour what it already is; the absolute purity, brilliance, luminescence, pearlescence, gift that the canvas itself is.

We asked you to look at the canvas which you are, and honour what is there; letting go again of the thoughts, beliefs, understandings, knowings, and open again to the beauty, magnitude of perfection and interconnected Wholeness/Oneness that is: that just is. And coming from this space - many call the inside or inner world - letting go of, again, any preconceived cognitive notions, and being in wonder and awe of what is here. It is a place we invite you to return to again and again and again, knowing that every time, the canvas itself is honoured and loved and embodied, for that is the metaphor we are using - the canvas lightens. You are already the perfect perfection that is.

When you return to this place within, every time it may be

unique, every time it may be different, and yet there may
be similar qualities and things you experience. You may
come to know this as an aspect of you, of self, of Big Self,
that is interconnected with all that is. For separation does
not exist. Yes, it is experienced but it does not truly exist.
We are very grateful to answer this most beautiful and
beauteous question. Thank you.

Thank you! Part of me wants to ask who came in to answer
the question and another part of me is just in such honour
for the answer, so thank you and I will carry on with the
next question. The next question is this:

HOW CAN I ALLOW MY EXPERIENCE OF SEPARATION TO
LOOSEN?

(Well, it seems like that question was already answered but
I will still pose that question as a possibility for another
answer or more illumination from another vantage point of
the same.)

I would like to answer this question, again, from another
vantage point, so it can be heard in another capacity. And
our answer is this; to loosen what it is that you think that
you are, that you think that you are aware of, is to loosen
all connections. And many of those are found at this time
within your heart, within that energetic space that you
may feel within your chest. Beautiful dear ones, this is
more sacred than we could ever fully communicate to you
through your language at this time, so please move your
awareness in any way you can to this heart space.

If you don't feel or experience anything, that is fine;
it is just placing your awareness in this space as we

communicate to you, through you. This heart space has become very full in your experience here as Humanity, here on this planet called Earth. There have been many vibrations put into effect or play, so that this center is having the experience it is. Some may feel it as heavy; some may feel it as painful; some may feel it as closed off. These are just sensations and we invite you now to allow those vibrations that, to this point in time, have been experienced in some way or another, to be released. For it is you, the chooser, in this lifetime, in this embodying of a body, that chooses what comes next, by choosing what happens now. We are here at all times, for anyone who will hear, or read, or experience this transmission. We will always be here to assist anyone, anytime, of loosening - if you so choose - the vibrations that are occurring through the heart space. As we have your permission, we choose to assist you.

And so, we will take the next couple of moments, seen here as a pause, to do just that. In your allowing and receiving of us, which truly is another aspect of the All That Is, which you are, we are here to assist and serve each of you uniquely and individually, in releasing that which no longer serves. And you may know what this is, and yet we still invite you to open up into that space of wonderment that was described in the question earlier, to truly open in childlike wonder. And in that space of openness it is easy, it is simple, for us to assist with your request. The fear is not here, the anger is not here, it is released in that childlike wonderment, that infinite space of creative knowingness. And so we begin.

Pause.

Allow yourself to breathe into that middle chest space.

Allow yourself to open in any way that feels right for you, in any ways that feel right to you.

Allow the energy and fluidity to just move.

Some may experience what feels like harmony, some may experience openness, some may experience joy, some bliss. These are all higher vibrations. We use this time, on your behalf, with your allowance and confirmation of that allowance, to gently, easily, productively, fluidly, and fully release this heart space. And the more often you allow yourself to be in this space of openness, of wonderment, that allows you, the experiencer, to move into higher and higher vibrational states. It is like taking a backstroke in water, gently, fluidly, easily, only instead you're doing this not laterally or horizontally, but vertically, up into higher spaces, maybe echelons, of vibration.

Just as the keys of a piano can move up into the higher vibrations, so can we, with our choosing. And we are overjoyed to have this opportunity to assist you in doing just that. For that is truly why we are here. Thank you ever so much and we will be with you anytime we are allowed the opening and opportunity to be with you. Gratitude!

Thank you, thank you for that beautiful explanation. I really feel that wholehearted, beyond 100% commitment to be there at every opportunity that each one of us can allow so, wow, thank you. I can definitely feel that in my heart, thank you.

So, I ask this third question now, wondering what the answer will be!

WHAT MORE ABOUT OUR ENERGY BODIES WOULD YOU LIKE US TO KNOW AND CAN YOU SHARE WITH US RIGHT NOW?

I hope the question is clear enough and yes it seems it is, the energies are coming in.

Inbreath.

Oh, beautiful, beautiful, beautiful, beautiful dear, so-called, embodied ones. I will use, for the sake and ease that you are in a body, for you believe that you are embodied, and it is not yet time for the conversation that you are not. Many of you so believe you are embodied that we honour the belief system we come in with, we honour the parameters in which we will be communicating with you through. What we would like to do now is to take this window of opportunity and be with the bodies, guiding you through the words that this dear one has allowed us to borrow, to utilize.

So, we would like you to become aware of any and all sensations that you are having, through what you think of as your body. And we will start there, for there is energy, there is vibration that is moving through this - holographic patterning - would be a more apt way of communicating what it is you perceive your body as being. And as this is happening, please note, and do not be afraid, that we are working on expanding the awareness and the edges of what you perceive as your body.

You can always revert back to an older idea of what the body is. We are here to gift you an expanded version of what that is. Take this as whatever it is that you can and that you choose. The gift is yours to do with as you choose, as it always is. We just really enjoy the opportunity to zoom out the lens and allow your awareness of what is to become larger, if only for a moment.

As the spaces and definitions become blurred between what you see as inner and what you see as outer transpires, we would like to be with certain aspects of the body, for the sides, as in what you experience as left and right are expanding; so too are what is backward and forward, or front and back for you. So is the experience of up and down or upper and lower, so too is within and without. For they are all gradients of the same, they are all Oneness and Wholeness, here for you to create with and through.

Feel free to breathe as deeply and fully and in what is the most supportive for you, as this will enliven and really animate the energetics of this patterning, of this body. As this is happening, there is a greater allowance for shifting within the patterning itself: within the energies that are your so-called bodies. Breathe into any spaces that may be denser and that you may feel as so-called troubling; your areas where you have held energies that may not be moving as freely or smoothly in this patterning. It is all loved by us, for it is all love, and whatever you are ready to hand over, that you know it is time because you've had a full experience of whatever it is you are experiencing, let go. We are now allowed to assist in your releasing of this, for we are an aspect of you as you are an aspect of us.

There is so much joy in being with you in any, and every capacity we have. We so love these bodies, these patterns of energy. We so love them. We are no longer in experience of them and yet we so love them. They are like a beautiful gift, beautiful stars in the sky, diamonds and sparkly jewels in a cave. And again, all patterning, all joyous celebration of what is within, is also expressed externally.

And now allow for even more movement to gently and easily take place, to happen, to allow us to intermingle and merge in the correct capacity for you, through your higher awareness, because that is what we are following. It is very much your guidance to us. Some of it is what you experience as your mind; much of it is your heart and your higher vibrational guidance. And to these questions in this chapter, it is the attempt of this seeker and knower, to allow for these higher vibrational capacities to become available for you. That has always been her concern. For in that she is in honour, love, and bliss. That is her calling, whether she is aware of that or not. And so, we easily move through her energetic patterning, to gift this to you, for you to have in a way that is absolutely perfect and complete. We are able to do this; we are aspects of your higher vibration, here to gift, and in some cases, to guide you now, back to that which you choose, which is in service and is perfect for you in this moment.

And the energies have been moving the entire time

that we have been in communication with you. And this moment is almost complete and yet the vibrations are always accessible at any moment, for there is no time, no place, no space. And yet there is through your awesome, infinite capacity to create this experience of body, of time, of place, of space, and we honour that so fully. It is such a beautiful expression of the Divine. And with that we know that this is complete. Return as often as you choose for us to be of service with you. Thank you, dear beautiful loved ones, and so it is.

So, my fourth question to the energies that are all around us...

WHAT DO YOU SEE AS OUR NEXT STEPS TO CREATING AND EMBODYING THE WHOLENESS AND ONENESS WE ARE?

(Well again it seems like that was already answered in the last question, but I'm still very excited and always game to see what comes through as an answer in creating and embodying the Wholeness and Oneness we are. It seems like this is a very old and ancient energy that is coming through our timeline.)

Oh child, we have been waiting for what seems like eons, and yet, paradoxically, no time, for this opportunity to be with you, to be embodied by you, flowing through your energy system. We are here with purpose. We are here at this absolute perfect, and truly divinely planned, intersection of time. You called us into being many, many, many ages ago when you, this embodied being, were part of us. And we know you are remembering this throughout your entire system, and yes, it is full of emotion as it is full of a returning love that you have not experienced since that time signature. And we will wait as this equilibrates itself through your experience.

We are here in your energetic system and field to finally be ready to assist all others in their own remembrance of what it is they called into play and place in this now - capable and ripe and nourishing and nutrient-filled, time-space place. We are experiencing each one of you individuated and as a whole; as we are all a whole, no longer individuated. We understand, as in, can see why, compute, and understand your choosing of separation and yet in our presence we are gifting you the remembrance of the Wholeness and Oneness that you also are. And as we do this, we ask of you to allow the deep remembrance that you are, that you always have been, no matter what you have played with, no matter what you have experienced, to return. You have always been a part of this Wholeness, no matter what vibrational experience you have of it. You have always also been it, no matter how far into separation you have gone for the pure joy of the experience. The human experiencer may not have experienced it as joy, but you did it for the experience, because you could. We so honour that. And we call you back into the remembrance of what it is that you are, that we are, that is. We call this remembrance back into every atom, into every subatomic particle that you will never get to the bottom of dear scientists and dear ones: for it is never-ending and never beginning. Which is the same as you, as above, so below; as below, so above. There is no start or end to any of it. There never has been. You have experienced it as such and there never has been.

And the mind will say, "How can I experience something that has never been?". You are the ultimate master creator, Divine Master Creator. Of course, the Multiverse says yes to every vibration that you put out there, through the heart, through the mind, that you are experiencing through any other vibrational capacity. The universe steps up and says, "Yes, we will give you that." No matter if it's heartache, no matter if it is confusion, no matter if it is separation. It took you a very long time to get to this point of separation and you so excelled at every step. And now we hear your call to return back from this wonderful experience of separation, of duality, back into the Wholeness and Oneness that you have always been, and you decide how far you move back into that.

We can hear, "Is it possible to do this in one lifetime?" Absolutely, it is possible to do instantaneously. Whether you will or not is up to you. We still detect fears, we still detect disturbances in your energetic field. And that is honoured. And it is your choice to come into harmony with those fears or not. For you already are, it's just your experience to move back into your allowance of yourself, to let go of what you have experienced. And yes, it is simple, and yes, it is easy, and yes, it is just a choice away. For there are very strong vibrations all around you ready to assist. So, you choose; so all choose. And those that are ready, when they are ready, move further and further into the flow of the Wholeness and the Oneness that is. We have been here the entire time waiting to embrace you, and receive our loving aspects of ourselves back, when, and as, and how, you are ready. Make the call and the choice, for we are already here. And so it is. With so much love and gratitude. Thank you.

So, my fifth question is...

WHY ARE WE HAVING THE EXPERIENCE OF A PHYSICAL BODY OF DENSITY AND DUALITY WHEN SO MANY NO LONGER SEEM INTERESTED IN THIS EXPERIENCE? IS THERE AN EVOLUTIONARY ASPECT TO THIS?

We see that you have come across this aspect of your evolution. And this one is less clear to be able to describe to you as you are in the third dimension and the answer is not. There are so many aspects to this idea of evolution that go far beyond any part of the known description of this word. We will do our best to communicate what this evolutionary aspect of the duality that you are experiencing is. Many have heard stories of this evolution. Some include different incarnations; some include multiple types or times of evolution that maybe Humanity did not succeed in arising from the duality or density. That, we would like to set aside as a story for now and explain in this fashion:

Move all of your awareness into this now moment. Allow all the energies that you are to move into this present now moment. Centering again, and as that starts to happen, allow the mind to soften and the body to be. It just happens. It just happens. And as we say this, moment by moment, it is evolution. Evolution is the want, desire, and answer; to shift, to change, to move into another vibrational state. The planet has done this many times. She herself is a master. And yes, you are feeling that nudge to go through this experience yet again. So just as the analogy of a crystal being a high vibrational capacity of what you call rock or stone, as a flower is a higher reaching aspect of the plant, so too you are being asked to move again into another capacity.

The bodies are already underway in this capacity, shifting and changing energetically in unison with the vibrational requests or asks that are non-verbal. They are just energy. And the bodies are doing a fantastic job of this. As they are flowing, energy is responding and now we ask that the mind, the personality, some use the word ego, also follow suit. And time and again, it is by letting go and receiving again what is, in a very open and described to you as a child-like manner. You have experienced this in your youth, before you moved into concept and conceptualization, before this was taught to you. Allow yourself to return to that open space and state, whereby energies move easily, ideas and beliefs are soft, and no longer haggle in the mind, are no longer created from, are no longer bestowed upon anyone or anything. There is no description or need to describe or analyze or categorize, just being with all that is; all that is around and all that is within. For it is in this place of withinness that you start to truly shine, to vibrate your Truth. And we say Truth with a capital T as it is this full capacity, it is this universal resonance that radiates as energy, pure energy, through the body.

And why have you come in the form of a body? That was part of the package, part of the deal or experience that you chose, that you knew was here as a potential because, there are many potentials and many timelines, in many dimensions, in many vibrational capacities. And your awareness landed here, to experience that which it wanted, which it could partake in. And not from a place of the mind, not from the place of personality or ego, but truly from the place and space of wonderment. Imagine an all-knowing child being able to look down or experience and know that there was a place it could sneak itself into, a far vestigial corner in which to play, in which to play a game it thought it did not know what it was. It is exciting for the soul, for this aspect of you, to have that experience. There aren't many avenues or areas where this can be experienced or performed. And so, you find yourself here, all the while being called back now.

So absolutely, parts of you no longer want to be in form because you know you are being called back out of the type of vibration or form that you have been within. And this is okay. But it is part of your linear process. The answer was spoken earlier that yes, this could be done instantaneously and yet many of the agreements that are part of being here are for a linear unfoldment. Some do not play by this rule any longer. Some know deeply and fully and remember that it is a vibrational experience. And so, moving through the vibrations consciously, they are able to move out of the game: letting go of the need for physical form while being in form and no, not deceasing or dying, which is a common experience here, but moving out of form. As some of your stories of Jesus explain, moving out of form- resurrecting is the word.

And yet there is no body, for there is no body to begin with. Some may experience the corporeal shell or husk, others will not, again, depending on their vibrational fluidity. When you are in that lower vibration and experiencing the physical form, it is there for your enjoyment in some ways, as a true vehicle is there to transport you, knowing all the while the body is waiting for your queues, your understandings, your a-ha's, your knowings, your openness and acceptance to take that next step, to blossom into what it has always been designed to be.

There is a feeling of frustration and stuckness on this planet as each one of you move through what has been described as the eye of a needle. And what can go through the eye of a needle? Not much. But, by rarifying further and further, the vibrations are rarifying further and further to allow you to come out the other side as what it is that you are and enter another evolutionary and vibrational state. Do all need to go there? No. But those that choose so, will enter another called-into space of experience. We hope this makes sense to you in some way, capacity, or form.

Thank you for the question and the ability to take the time for us to answer as best we could. Goodbye.

And so, the sixth question I have to ask is this...

WHEN WE RE-EXPERIENCE THE SEPARATION OR THAT LOWER VIBRATIONAL EXPERIENCE, HOW CAN WE MORE COMFORTABLY OR CONSCIOUSLY BE WITH THAT?

We hear what you are asking to have answered and yet we feel that we will not be answering it in the way that may have been expected or thought. When you move into the lower vibrational experiences, it is its own experience. There are their own emotions, their own thoughts and ideas and beliefs, that live, and truly live, and are resonant

171

with those vibrations. And we would like to say that while those are around and available to you in these lower vibrational energy states, there is always the possibility of being aware of them, the emotions, and thoughts, the ideas, the patterns; and yet there is always the ability - through intent, through choice - to keep moving to a higher echelon or vibrational state. That is where your free will comes in, your choice. And it takes a conscious, concerted effort to be with the content, the vibrations when you're there and relaxing within them, knowing that they are transitionary, that you are not 'stuck' in them, they do not 'have' you. That's just part of the back and forth, the flow, like a wave in and out of the ocean, until you are ready to no longer be within the wave but to be the ocean.

And at times you have had those experiences. And yes, it is similar and akin to exercising a muscle. And yet, beautiful souls, you also have it within you right now to access these higher states at any time. We would like to show you that, as we have stated, time does not exist. So, allow the knowing that you may experience linearly to come into this now moment. What it is that you will experience to be here now, in whatever way serves you fully and completely, just let that happen now. The mind may know something of this and yet the body is a true Master, for it is always in the present moment. It cannot exist in this capacity outside of this now. Letting all aspects of this that you are, move into this now, giving your yes, your agreement of all that it is that serves you to remember and know about maintaining or staying at a higher vibrational capacity; one that you choose and one that serves you, that your soul is in resonance with. There are many and you are a part of that choice and choosing.

The concepts are not simple, straightforward or linear. There are many aspects to moving into and attaining higher vibrational states. And know that it will happen without any conscious choice on your part. For those of you that choose to be the forerunners, and that is you: those that are interested, that ride the first energetic waves forward, that are compelled forward (you know who you are), it is opening yourself up freely, allowing the energy to flow through you and to flow to you, and to allow those possibilities to be here on the planet. For just as one individuated individual experiences one thing, so it is available for all.

And it is not about doing your homework - it's about following your passion and bliss; it's about becoming that deep within yourself and allowing that which is deep within yourself to come forward. Again, another aspect of unity, a yes, a full vibrational coherence and adherence as they interlace into the Oneness that You Are.

Really it's about setting your choice, be that in time, be that in openness, in willingness, as often as you feel the tap/nudge, to choose to maybe not move into a lower vibration of victimization, to know that you are in choice. And please know, it does not matter to us where it is on that scale of vibration you are, it is all love. We do love you regardless of anything you could ever do. There is no thing that could ever be done that would stop us (chuckle) from loving you, we cannot do such a thing. That is just an experience of the separation that the child experienced in the corner. Separation does not exist. We are always here with you. But at this point in time we are with you in moments of choice, we are with your conscious awareness at times when you choose to remember and invite the vibrational remembrances of yourself in, when you choose to gift yourself with yourself in whatever means that is.

We know this is, again, not the clearest answer but it is the most fluid and truthful we can gift to you now. Thank you for allowing us to have you as an open-hearted audience of receivership, of the love that We All Are. Blessed be beautiful ones and then we step back.

My final question is this, which again seems like it's been answered many times...

PLEASE SHARE A FEW SIMPLE STEPS IN RETURNING TO UNITY CONSCIOUSNESS.

We start with the definition of what Unity Consciousness is. For unity is Wholeness, is One. And that is best experienced through the center of the body, through the heart. Unity Consciousness is every aspect of every energy and it is through your brilliance that you have been able to experience separation from the unity, from the Wholeness, into separate vibrations of experience. The vast majority of the energies are in this unity experience. As energy expands, it is more on the edges and fringes that the separation exists. And so, pulling back again to the center, into your center, into your core, yes into your heart, is one way, an aspect to step back into Unity Consciousness.

So too is spending time out in what you call nature, where there is vibrational balance. For that is the normal. Like we said, it is the almost constant throughout the universe:

walking into a forest, walking into a field, spending time in the ocean or lakes, waters, moving up into the freedom of the air, deep within a cave, the tops of mountains. In these locations, in climbing a tree, dear ones, this puts you back into the remembrance of Unity Consciousness, of wholeness, of balance, of fullness. The return to Unity Consciousness is only a thought, a breath away; it is a choice away.

This can be done through meditation, relaxation, joy. We do not go looking for this, it occurs, for it is what is natural: as natural as a baby's breath and a baby's cry. Your feeling or experience of wholeness and unity becomes fuller and more resonant as you move into a state of chosen balance. Like we said, this happens naturally, all the time, and would happen much more frequently if the mind weren't off protecting you, or saving you, in a story of some sort or some kind of your making; the mind entrapment, enslavement, which is honoured and which, day by day, hour by hour, moment by moment, loosens. This is just what it is, this is just the trajectory that you are on.

And so, it becomes easier with time to let go of the mind and the games. There are wonderful ways such as eating well or clean, consuming fresh water, being in places of openness, staring at the clouds in the sky, loose eye focus, watching the skies at night, staring into a fire, watching the sunset. These moments of softness, these moments of aliveness, these moments where there are no differences or differentiation between what is within and what is without. There never has been. And it is through your setting aside of your experience of time, placing it where you choose, for you are doing that all the time whether you are aware of it or not, you can access or open or come into Oneness again in your awareness, of the unity, the part and parcel, the piece that really is the Wholeness and Oneness of All. It's merely a breath away, a smile away, a choice away. And we wish you the absolute, most profound success in your endeavours, in your path, in your choices. And we just are so full of gratitude for being here with you now.

Thank you for your time, for your patience, for your awareness, of centering and remembering your Divine Self, your Divinity, your wholeness and fullness and trueness. It's what we love, it's what we are, and it's what We All Are. Blessings beautiful souls. Good-bye.

I also wondered if there were any questions and answers or information you wanted to give that maybe my questions had not covered or pointed to or allowed to be illunimated. I give this time now for anything that wants to come forward. Thank you.

We are honoured to be given the opportunity to share with you the information that we have the ability to gift to you now. And as we say this, there is much in the way of energy that is pouring forth and through all around you. There are many sacred geometrical shapes, there are many vibrational signatures, many wavelengths, many patternings of energies that are gifting the bodies, the beings, the souls. Many of this is very rich in what you would experience as life force energy, and it is through this vessel of a being that this energy can be transduced, can be stepped down, can be received onto the planet. And we ask you in this moment to tap into what that is through your awareness, that you are capable and here, and can and choose to receive now.

For it is all around you, wordless and nameless, for there are no words to give this at this time. Just open and receive the multitude upon multitude of gifts that are here to be bestowed on you. So beautiful, so loved, so Love. Receiving that in anyway possible, every way possible, letting it seep deep into your bones, letting it lightly caress the cell walls, to seep into the fascia in your body, to illuminate the neurons that flow and course through the body, to move through the electrical system, and open the bandwidth of what it is that's possible for you to receive. Yes, exactly that, opening to receive, opening in wonderment, opening in agreement, opening in happiness and joy. Yes. Because with your yes and opening, more can flow through, more can be received into the vessel that you are, and yes you are infinite and experiencing still a form of limitation.

It has changed over the course of time; it has expanded, and you are expanding again to receive even more of what it is you are. And we are so overjoyed by this. It is so beautiful. We wish we could describe to you what it is that we experience, in words, and yet there are no words for us to use. So, we send you the vibration in any and every way possible for you to receive at anytime, anywhere, through your choosing. Just let it flow through in any way, shape, and form you can. This is one of our favorite parts of being with you, the gifting of You to you, the gifting of You through you. We so love you. And we know it is now time to let go, and to have our own experience, to maybe close the portal of access, allowing you to have your experience. Again, we are so grateful for this time together. It is so special to us, as are you. A million thank-yous. And so it is.

And so it is.

Arianna's Summation: For it is you, the Chooser, in this lifetime, in this embodying of a body, that chooses what comes next, by choosing what happens now. We are here at all times, for anyone who will hear, or read, or experience this transmission.

ARIANNA'S STORY

This beautiful human has had many experiences leading up to this channeled chapter, that have assisted her in being capable and able to perform this endeavour. Make no mistake; it has taken dedication and commitment on her part to be in a capacity in which to allow the energies and interpretations of them for the chapter. She has honoured many of the tasks and challenges that have come her way and she continues to feel, grow, and expand into more, as so many of you dear readers are in the process of doing as well. We congratulate you throughout each and every step you take, we celebrate your courage, bravery, and self-discipline, as that is what is required of you in many ways. Know that we love you dearly and deeply, for you are our family, you are each a part of what it is We Are.

In love and joy,

The Universe

During the 43 cycles Arianna has been traveling with our Solar System, she has had the joy of experiencing friendship, travel, expansion, and expression. She has enjoyed and appreciated many aspects of her life, including graduating university with a B.Sc. in Zoology, living in the Northwest Territories and working as a biologist for the government, getting married and having a family (including two phenomenal daughters and multiple fur companions), and opening and remembering her energetic abilities. She has especially loved sharing those knowings and abilities with others and in assisting others in opening their knowings and abilities.

She currently lives in Elora, Ontario, and enjoys continually expanding into more freedom, remembrance, and Being the Divinity We Are.

Arianna Zimmer

Website: www.shootingstarenergies.com
Email: shootingstarenergies@gmail.com
Facebook: www.facebook.com/shootingstarenergies

CHAPTER 7

HUMANITY'S ADJUSTMENT

Creating Peace on Earth

by Bonnie Bogner
Wisdom of the Galactic Council

G reetings dear ones, we are the Council and it is with great joy that we step into your presence. We wish to speak to you about a number of different topics, yet all related as they tie closely to the vast changes that are happening upon your planet at this time and the journey it has been for humanity to adjust to them.

LIFE CHOICES

We will begin the exploration with Life Choices. Why it is that you chose a certain experience or set of circumstances?

You see, each soul is at a different level of evolution, and therefore, needing to select different experiences. Even those experiences and what it is that you will learn from them will vary depending upon the age of that soul. If a soul has a difficult experience, say with starvation and they are a very young soul, they are learning in the lower chakras about survival. Their soul learns and grows through that experience, which goes into their storehouse or Akash. That soul continues to grow, expand and learn, and many lifetimes later they choose to have another experience with starvation. This experience may relate to cellular memory they are healing from the first experience if they have not yet released the trauma associated with starvation. Or they may be using starvation to experience something in the upper chakras such as compassion for themselves or others who are starving, maybe gratitude for those who come to their aid, or compassion for those who have the means to help but do not for whatever reason. There are so many possibilities of what each experience may be about. Suffice to say, the lessons will be different each time, even if the circumstances are similar. Such is the complexity of selecting circumstances.

Each experience is chosen as an opportunity to learn and to grow, not chosen simply to make life seem unbearable. We understand that is what much of humanity thinks; that difficult things are put in their lives by someone else, including God, specifically to make life difficult or unbearable.

You see, from your soul's perspective, there is nothing unbearable; only opportunity to learn. That does not mean that we are condoning the experience of extreme pain, or that the more pain that you have, the more that you learn and grow. There is an element of truth to that, for you would not have gotten to the place you are if you had no challenges or no difficulties. However, there is also the opportunity to learn from a more gentle, joyful place. Some of what is coming upon this planet is a great opportunity for things to be more gentle.

There are many that are still completely committed to learning from fear and pain, so they will be searching for the most difficult of circumstances. Then there are those who simply refuse to learn what it is that they have come to learn so they continue to repeat and repeat and repeat difficult experiences. Finally, there are those who will go through some difficulty and will decide there must be a better way, choose to look at things differently than they did in the past, and also be determined to improve their life. This will provide the opportunity for life to get better and learning to become more comfortable. **This is creation.**

Please understand, dear ones, that you do not just come here to learn. You are also part of a much larger construct; it is a complex and beautiful system that has been put in place for each one of you, not just to learn, but also to teach. This process helps each one of you, as you are simultaneously the student and the teacher. **This is co-creation.**

There are many upon this planet who facilitate healing, who refer to themselves as spiritual teachers and that is not the role that we are referring to. They are indeed spiritual teachers and their role is vital. But we wish to take the understanding of teacher a step further. What we are suggesting is that every single being upon the planet has something to teach someone or several others. And every single being upon the planet has much to learn, often from the most challenging of relationships. You would not come into physical incarnations unless you were choosing to have an opportunity for your soul to grow and evolve.

We know there are also those upon the planet who feel that they are ascended beings who wonder what they are doing here in physical form, having what appears to be difficult lessons. Just because someone has successfully gone through the maze once it does not mean there is no more appeal or opportunity within the maze. Each maze may have several possible solutions and why would a curious soul not want to try them all? The successful completion of the maze could be equated to ascension with different learnings, expansion, and outcomes for that soul each time through.

It is all beautiful and appropriate, not designed for you to fail, or simply as a painful experience as some believe. For you see, the more you are able to be in a place of observation and evaluation, the less you need to take the experiences personally. The more that you can learn from challenges and observe them, the greater the opportunity to choose a different reaction next time and have a completely different path through the maze. It is such a beautiful experience, a complex unfolding, that was designed specifically for this dimension and the specific group of lessons that humanity is calling forth. You see there are other lessons and experiences upon other planets and in other dimensions. They are not better or lesser than; they are simply different. Many experiences are not repeatable from dimension to dimension as everything behaves differently in each one.

What we would invite you to do, is begin to think about the possibility of your experiences being a grand opportunity for you to learn and grow, rather than a punishment or karmic payback put upon you because you were somehow bad, wrong or unsavoury in another life.

The only karmic payback from life to life is that you need to heal something that you are carrying around within your soul's imprint. That does not mean you are being punished for that life, rather that you have not yet figured out and released what is hampering you. There is much that can hamper, but also much than can be healed.

It is now time to embark upon the healing, look for the good, the gold and the opportunity in experiences. To stop beating yourself up when it has nothing to do with you being good or bad and has everything to do with what you are here to learn. Permit yourself to learn from that which you experience, and to choose a different response, if the way you have been responding does not suit you. If you are playing the role of victim and you enjoy being that victim, then, by all means, continue to play that role. But if you are experiencing yourself in victimization and it does not feel good to you, it does not fit well anymore, then we would invite you to make a clear commitment to yourself that you will no longer play that role. This is not magic; this is commitment; this is clarity. Many who are victims enjoy being victims because they think it somehow justifies their pain. In reality, all it does is exacerbate that pain. Give yourself permission to step out of the pain, to step out of the victimization, and to choose to be empowered to be your own director and learn what you came to learn. Look with a positive outlook and aspect upon the potentials. Choose for it to be different and commit to that choice.

This does not mean all will become immediately and instantly perfect, rather it will send a clear signal to the universe that you are serious about learning what you came to learn and responding in the most positive way possible.

We are here to support you in every step of your journey, just as all of your non-physical team are, but we can only assist when we are invited and allowed to. Please invite us to help and allow us to do so.

'NON-CONFORMING' GENDER IDENTITY

We now wish to speak to you of a topic that has been providing significant confusion and polarization for so many upon the planet, the ones of gender identity and sexuality.

We wish to acknowledge in advance that we may not use all the terminology that each one of you considers proper upon your planet. This is in no way intended as disrespect, we see you all as perfect in whatever form you are and celebrate whatever terms you use. In truth, the terminology you use is irrelevant to us as we see all of you as beautiful souls. Being called he, she, it, or they does not change our perspective or love for you.

This unfolding of gender identity has been providing a great opportunity for you to learn, and it has also been providing an opportunity for much frustration and confusion and pain.

It is only in a world of duality, which we have already spoken of, in which you can have two clearly defined extremes of sexual identity. In this case, you have identified them as male and female. In truth, none of you is completely male or completely female. You all have the completeness of energy; you couldn't survive without it. You must have the masculine and the feminine energies in some combination. We know that you have your scientific studies that prove there is a certain gene combination that makes a male or a female and how that cannot be varied. That is only a third-dimensional test, where you are multi-dimensional beings. We are also delighted that not all scientists continue to agree with those limited findings.

There is much operating beyond the third dimension that influences your experiences and your energy. It is actually your multi-dimensional energy profile that is determining this identity that you are confused about. You have created two aspects that are in contrast as the bookends of the entire experience. More and more people are now waking up to the range of experience, not just one extreme or the other.

For those that are committed to the extremes of the experience, this creates fear and confusion for they do not know how to operate or how to process anything in between. Many are now trying to comprehend that range between the extremes, with varying degrees of success. Think of someone who is colour blind and can only see black and white. They simply cannot see green or blue no matter how hard they try. They may understand the theory of green and blue existing but have no frame of reference for those colours. This limits their ability to understand what it would be like to see those colours. Just as those who have only ever operated from one extreme or the other, they may understand there is much in between, but have little ability to truly comprehend what it would be like to be somewhere in between.

Those who have no direct frame of reference will react from a place of attempted comprehension and compassion, or from a place of fear. In that place of fear, they direct their inability to understand towards those who are triggering the fear, often in the form of anger. We are not suggesting this is acceptable, simply stating what is occurring. Those operating from compassion are still limited in their response, but at least they are attempting to understand.

Those not residing at the extremes are somewhere within the spectrum and helping bring the world to a new place of understanding. They have been told they should pick one of the extremes and adapt, which creates much discomfort and confusion for them. They feel that they are not fulfilling what others expect of them as they are compelled to something different, yet many cannot completely identify their knowing. So, there is a grand opportunity for them as they learn to embrace their multi-dimensional energetic profile and stand in their truth, regardless of that truth making sense to those at the extremes.

Add to all of this, the current pattern that humans expect other humans adhere to, such as the strict rules for the appearance of the body and its adornments, which actually makes no sense. Why should you not wear whatever adornments that create comfort and provide functionality? Rules about what clothes should and should not be worn are purely human-made and truly serve little purpose except to limit you.

This is an unfolding process that is going to continue, and it will become easier in the coming years. The older

generations upon the planet have very little frame
of reference for this new way of being. The younger
generations have been born into this new energy and
awareness; therefore, the frame of reference is different.
With each successive generation, there will be a greater
and greater comprehension of the full spectrum and it
will become easier.

Some have chosen to have these full-spectrum gender
experiences for their own lessons and learnings. Others
have chosen this route specifically as teachers. There are
many ascended beings upon the planet who are choosing
to have these gender differences specifically to teach
others about the completeness of energy, rather than the
polarization of it.

There are also those who are transitioning from lives as
one sex to lives as the other (e.g. moving from male to
female experiences) and it may take a couple of mixed
identity lives to fully make that transition. While this has
been a factor since the beginning of time, this is not what
has caused this massive shift upon the planet in these
past years. If you think of two or three hundred years ago,
there was not yet an entire range of gender expressing
as has now been presented. This width and depth of
possibility simply did not exist then as it does now.

As you continue moving out of the extremes, many will
explore this range in between. This is just one of the
areas where this shift is showing up, and it will take
humanity some time to sort it out. As we said, it will come
through the generations as more and more are born
into understanding these new energy concepts. At some
point, it will simply become a non-issue, and souls will

be accepted in whatever body experience they choose to have. And finally, at some point humanity will look back with amazement at the dichotomy that there was upon the planet and how it created fear and divided people.

Know, dear ones you may be feeling trapped in between these extremes or you may be feeling righteous in your position at an extreme. It does not matter whereabouts within the spectrum you are. You are all contributing to this awakening in your own way and you are all having the opportunity to learn exactly what you need to from this process.

What we would suggest to you, is that you be kind and gentle to yourself in whatever your identity is and that you be kind and gentle with your neighbour in whatever their identity is. Do not try to explain it away or figure it all out. Simply be present with the fact that what you are experiencing may be different than what society says and what your neighbour is experiencing may be different than what you experience.

This is, in some ways, a metaphor for all that is going on upon the planet at this time. The extremes are being blurred and blended into the middle. That is how this new way of being and experiencing comes about.

It is appropriate for the shifting that is happening at this time, and it will continue to unfold in new and unexpected ways. So those of you who are feeling resistance to this, you may as well learn to accept it! Your choosing a state of resistance is not going to make it go away, it is simply going to make your life uncomfortable as the changes continue to unfold.

ANXIETY AND DEPRESSION

I*t is time now for us to speak to you about a topic that has been acquiring much attention of late. That is the topic of mental health, specifically the area of anxiety and depression.*

Disclaimer

We do **not** profess to be medical professionals offering any medical advice. We encourage anyone experiencing anxiety, depression or any other symptoms to seek the assistance of their health care provider. This information is intended only as an understanding of the multidimensional.

For those of you that are reading that are over 50 years old, you may not have even heard the term anxiety until later in your years. Some of that was because it simply wasn't spoken of, and some is due to the fact it was much less common than now. There are reasons for that which we will explore in a moment.

Depression used to be a dark and dirty secret. You were not to speak of it. You were to hide people away if they had what is now classified as depression.

Both of these, as well as other neurological symptoms that make it difficult to function in the world, are actually part of the awakening lessons and learning that are now occurring upon the planet. You see, there is great learning that occurs within these experiences. This is also true of many of the currently recognized conditions labelled as disorders or syndromes. They are groups of lessons and learning opportunities that have become prevalent upon the planet, so much so that they have acquired their own labels.

For now, we will focus upon these two specific areas known as anxiety and depression, as most who are learning from the entire range of neurological symptoms will experience one or both of these as part of their journey.

The best we could describe something like anxiety is that it is a rushing of the thought process. The mind moves into overdrive and therefore it rushes through the thoughts and the possibilities so quickly that they cannot be settled and rectified as they come forth. So then, these thoughts all pile up one upon the other and they become this big mess of energy that results in the experience that you refer to as anxiety.

Think of each one of your thoughts as a car. When they are all driving on the highway in an orderly fashion following the speed limit, obeying the traffic signals and paying attention to where they are going, all is well. If that same group of cars decided to race, and all raced down the highway, out of control, not watching for other cars or traffic signals, and no longer paid attention to one another or traffic safety, it would not be long until accidents would begin to occur.

All your thoughts are those cars, all rushing headlong into the future until there is a crash or pileup. That is an anxiety attack. So many of those thoughts have rushed so fast and become so out of control it seems impossible to slow them down. And as you live in a world that praises rapid thought, rapid action, highly competitive business and productivity at all costs, the encouragement for those thoughts to move fast and to move out of control continues. When you were in a world that did not so highly prize multiple thought streams, multiple activities at the same time and humans gave themselves permission to simply sit and be present, there was much less out-of-control thought.

The inhabitants of this planet have access to so much more information than humanity is used to processing (think internet) as well as so many new potentials that never existed before. Add to that the loss of connection to the natural world for most people, and they are left with no way to ground and process all that is coming at them. The volume of information available to them is not the issue, rather that humanity has not yet learned how to be with all of it in a balanced manner.

Now, please understand, there is also a spiritual reason why this has happened. For in that speeding up, and the continued awakening, you are being presented with more and more to process. Some of this relates to the unfolding upon the planet that is putting pressure upon souls causing them to believe they must advance rapidly, rather than taking one thought, one step, another thought, another step.

There is the mistaken belief that if they take on all opportunities at once and try to carry through many experiences, many thoughts, many beliefs, many energies simultaneously, that they will somehow get there faster. While this may appear to be the best solution, it is simply not sustainable, hence the experience of anxiety. This headlong rushing of energy potential towards the elusive prize of awakening; the desire to find connection and home; and a lostness about where that might even be, all contribute to this experience.

Many souls, newly connected to the vast energy of awakening, have no idea how to slow the rush of potential, and in many cases do not wish to, as they believe the only way to truly become spiritual is to do it all at once. Or, they are not yet consciously connected to their spiritual awakening, so they have no frame of reference for what is happening to them. In the meantime, many simple tools practiced regularly can be beneficial. Things such as breathwork, meditation, walking in nature, quiet and reflective time, and getting enough sleep will all contribute tremendously.

Moderation is something that will be learned over time, and simply committing to a slowing of the frantic pace can help considerably. Part of that moderation is the recognition that one thing done towards awakening and done well is worth many, many half-done things, and is much easier on the nervous system.

The similar yet contrasting experience we wish to address is **depression.**

Where anxiety is this hurrying or rushing of energy towards the future; depression is this focus upon what was, a look into the past, and a belief or a desire to hold on to it. This stems from the mistaken belief that if you keep your pain near and dear, you will not repeat those mistakes. It is also reflective of the current opportunity presented upon this planet to wash away the past's emotional content. Many actually struggle with the possibility of letting past emotions go. Even as they profess their desire to release the Karmic Imprints of the past, they also wonder who they will be without all their badges of honour for pain and suffering. This is further amplified by the volume of past emotion that is being brought forward to be processed, from this life as well as from Karmic Imprints through the ages.

Anxiety and depression actually amplify one another. For that part of the being that believes that they need to focus on the past in order to not repeat mistakes, comes into conflict with that part of the person who wants to rush headlong into the future and process it all and get home. So that person then becomes exhausted with all that focus upon the past and all of that rushing to the future; soon left with zero capacity to be in the present. To simply be; that is one of the things that you came to do. That is the true path home, the true way to the self and the center is through the heart, through the self and through awareness.

While the origin and symptoms are different, the solutions for both are the same: connection, breath, centeredness and stillness. We understand that these are not easy to achieve once you are in this cycle of the rushing, the piling up, and anxious response to the future, compounded with the fear in looking back and holding onto the past. It is not necessarily easy to sit between the two and find that silence and space. If you could find the space for even one deep breath between the rush, the headlong movement into the future, and the heaviness of holding on to the past; even one breath in between begins to open or loosen each one.

Understand dear ones, it is not simply a matter of one breath or two or ten. It is a matter of cultivating a practice. In a society that believes the solutions lie within popping a pill or turning on a device to achieve some relief, there is very little patience and willingness to practice entering into your center and your breath in a way that will truly support you. This is best practiced when calm; the middle of an anxiety attack is not the best time to learn a new breathing pattern!

There are many different ways to enter into the space between. There is no one right breath pattern or activity. It is mindfulness and attention upon the breath. It is in the deepness of the breathing that oxygenation occurs in the body. It is the willingness to take that moment that is not in the past or the future and be present in it. It is that little crack between the past and the future where you are simply in this moment, in this now time.

If every time a person began to feel anxious, they could take even one moment, put their hand over their heart and breath right into their heart, even three breaths, they would help to soften that anxious feeling. If every time there was a focus upon the past and it was causing that heaviness or lethargy that comes with depression; if they took a moment to come into their heart, three breaths to let go of that past, even for a moment. With repetition and with practice, it would begin to move that person into the present moment, rather than rushing into the future or dragging along the past.

This may all seem too simple, and in the past, it may have been. But even as more and more potential for the future opens upon the planet, so too, does the potential to more easily and effortlessly release the past.

Many do not wish to believe it could be that easy. So, if they wish for it to be difficult, then they will be correct.

However, those that can begin to believe in a new paradigm, one of infinite potential and ease of release, they will almost appear to have superpowers in their ability to rapidly shift their reality.

We invite you to let the energy of the infinite potential flow through you, then simply catch the ideas that fit for you; do not grab and gather them all, many of those ideas are just passing by, not coming to you. Invite the new way of being to express itself with ease.

Choose to release the past and make it so; knowing you no longer require all of that in order to have an identity. You already have an identity as a beautiful divine soul, simply doing your best in this human experience.

Now, many other tools will support you in these experiences as well and we would encourage you to explore any or all that you may need to. So many of those tools will have limited effectiveness if they are not married with the breath, presence and centeredness in the moment. In that centering in the moment, the acknowledgement of self that you are Spirit, and that you have the right to take up space upon this planet. You are as great as the greatest and as small as the smallest, and that is enough. You are enough.

When you live in spirit there is no room for anything but your perfection. That is the state that you are moving towards at this time. Therefore, you are being crowded by these experiences called depression and anxiety because they are forcing you to find a way back into your center, back into your breath, and back into spirit. It is all perfect in its unfolding despite the discomfort that is created through those things. You truly are a society with an epidemic of anxiety and depression, which is the perfect place to learn from. But the time must be taken to learn, otherwise, the experience is simply painful. Some are learning from it, some are not, which is appropriate. Those that are learning from it will become the ones that will teach others. This will contribute to a slowing down and a centering of society, not just of the individual. That will contribute to where it is that humanity is choosing to go. It is all divine in the timing, in the execution, and in the potentials for the outcome.

IS IT MAGIC OR ALL JUST HOCUS POCUS?

It is now time for us to have a little chat with you about things that appears to be magical, mysterious or even impossible. There is much that is not yet understood, and that is appropriate, it is part of the mystery of your existence. If you already knew it all, what would be the fun in exploring?

And speaking of fun, let us first suggest the importance of humour. Spirit is not simply an exercise in seriousness. Spirit is also about levity, joy, and learning to laugh with yourself and with the world. This is not about making fun of, rather about not taking yourself too seriously. There are moments of humour sprinkled throughout your life if you take the time to notice them. Spirit and Spirituality are not all properness and challenges as some like to make it out to be. Spirituality is also the letting-go into genuine frivolity and humour.

So please take a moment, dear ones, and have a little laugh, a deep soul soothing belly laugh. Right now! Join us in laughter; you will be glad you did.

And now with this new lightness and personal connection that comes from laughter, we will address the main topic of this conversation. We love the term hocus pocus as there is an element of magic and joy to it, yet it is used by many to condemn what they do not understand.

There is also the misused term pseudoscience. You see, it is impossible for science to ever be ahead of Spirit's process of creation. For science cannot research what has not yet been revealed. As new creation occurs, or rather, as new awareness occurs, exploration is initiated. Many do not embrace the constantly expanding edges of your scientific knowledge or are committed to what has already been discovered. Science simply has not yet been fully explored, and in truth, never will be. Those hesitant to embrace new possibilities label what they do not understand in terms that they believe to be derogatory. However, there is no logic in using that term as an insult. For it is simply referring to something that you do not yet understand or believe. In order for it to have the term "science", it must have been researched, and yet this term pseudoscience is being used to make fun of those that are on the leading edge of expansion, therefore just beginning new research.

It is fine for them to have their experience and important to give honour to those that do not embrace the same beliefs as you. Even those that would label the sciences of intuition, channel, and energy healing, as hocus pocus or pseudoscience, have as much right to their opinion as you have to yours.

We are speaking of things such as our partner stepping aside so we can speak through her, those who speak to the deceased or angels, or those who create great change through the transmission of healing energy or casting of spells. This topic even encompasses ghosts, spontaneous healing, imagination and quantum physics.

How is it that those who create spells can change things? How can the healer send energy from afar and assist the person they are focused upon? Or, how can someone speak to the angels and receive guidance? All these things are occurring with great simplicity and order in the multidimensional, but you are only able to see the third-dimensional results, and from the purely 3D perspective, it may indeed appear to be hocus pocus!

Many would suggest that what you are doing is made up; or simply tricks, light shows or smoke and mirrors. We would like to assure you that nothing is further from the truth. When our partner is in a state of channel, she is deeply connected with her true and authentic self. She refers to that voice that comes through as Ye'Yesh Ye'Yar, which is the tone of her own awareness in its ascended state. We are speaking to her and through her simultaneously. We are separate and yet one with her. We are an individual and yet a collective. We understand much of this does not fit with your traditional definitions, yet many of you will intuitively understand exactly what we are speaking of.

You see, when she enters into this state of speaking with us, or of us speaking through her, she is moving into a state of surrender. When those that would cast spells or transmit healing energy go into their state of sacred ritual, they are in a state of surrender. When those that would do intuitive work, connecting to spirit guides, deceased loved ones or the angelic realm, they are surrendering and entering into a more vulnerable and open place. Each one is stepping out of their purely third-dimensional experience and into a multidimensional state.

This is a process of releasing the illusions of the third-dimension limitations and entering into the All That Is or the Greater Presence. Everyone, EVERYONE, who is in a third-dimensional body has the capacity to go into that multidimensional state. However, it requires a journey of believing that it can be so, and the willingness to surrender the illusion of your limitations.

When a soul is locked into linearity, that is all they can comprehend, and anything beyond that capacity may seem ridiculous. However, healing, intuition and imagination do not follow linear rules.

Without this surrender, there is no direct route to your authentic self and the sense of being home. Many use money or things to satisfy their craving and that is the birthplace of consumerism. Many use power-over-others and control to satisfy their craving and that is the birthplace of war. Still others use silence, stillness and surrender, and that is the birthplace of meditation. When action is added to the surrender, you have what is referred to as ritual. Ritual is meditation in action!

Yet this surrender creates fear for many. They see the great powers that seem to be bestowed upon those that would cast a spell, perform an unbelievable healing, or share wisdom from beyond. They see the anomalies that occur upon the planet that do not fit within the traditional understanding of the third dimension. Things such as the folding or expanding of time; tumours disappearing in moments, or rapid and miraculous shifts in circumstances. All of this defies the sciences of the third dimension and seems unbelievable, and in that lack of understanding is the fear.

You see, what is a standard experience in the multidimensional, appears to be impossible in the third dimension. And there are some strong oppositions to this, simply because it is not yet well understood. This started many eons ago when those who would do the healing work began to appear as a threat to those who did not understand. And rather than seeking answers, it was treated as a danger to be feared. Yet, ironically, most who truly understand that there is something more, have little interest in using it to dominate others. When you truly understand the beautiful and powerful being that you are, there is no need for power over others.

There are so many ways, so many possibilities of how vast healing can come about upon this planet. But before that healing can happen completely, the paradigm that everything is occurring in the third dimension must be shattered. So much of your experience is indeed in the multidimensional, being channelled through or routed into the third dimension where you can comprehend it. ALL of you are simultaneously having an experience here and beyond, even if you are not consciously aware of it. Yes, you are all channels of the higher dimensions, creating this third-dimension experience.

It is all as it should be. Many souls were calling for great and vast healing, and those souls have had their call answered. Some of them have been able to embrace that healing journey and some of them are still hesitant to do so.

We do not hold a vested interest in how, when, or where, you pursue your own personal healing. We rather hold an interest in peace upon this planet. For that peaceful place is where awakened awareness can grow. Ascension cannot grow in turmoil, conflict or dismissing of other's beliefs. There has been much pain inflicted upon this planet in the name of fear. There will continue to be more fear, as that is how some are still calling forth their growth. Humanity is progressing, but not completely done with its fear yet, and we honour that journey.

Humanity is also embracing peace, love and compassion. And for every person that makes that choice, the door is opened for more to choose. We are happy to assist in bringing a new light to this world, but we can only help you see and create what you are ready to receive. Big change and much healing are occurring at this time. There are so many through the ages that have contributed to that current healing and will continue to contribute to it. As each of you surrender and contribute to standing in your truth, you combine your light with so many others.

There is much beauty, and there is still pain and suffering, which is calling forth healing. We are here to help you learn to have this experience from a more peaceful place, that when accessed can allow peace, love and compassion to become your dominant force. **Soon that light of love and compassion will bathe the entire planet, and that**

will create peace on earth.

You are always at choice, what do you choose to create?

It is good that we have had this conversation with you today. It is important that you understand the reality of what lies beyond the dimension that you are in.

I am Ye'Yesh Ye'Yar of the Galactic Council, and so it is.

CONCLUSION

Love is the answer...now, what was the question?

Thank you, thank you, thank you!

Thank you for joining us on this adventure into love, light and oneness. We sincerely hope you found inspiration on these pages.

Thank you for showing up authentically in your own life, even when you struggled to know who that was.

And thank you for shining your light that others may find hope.

Writing this book has been a labour of love for all of us. It has also triggered our fears of being seen, heard and known as channels. What a beautiful gift! We have all had the opportunity to grow in this process.

NOW WHAT?

If these words have nurtured, healed or inspired you, we have accomplished what we set out to do. If any particular channel resonated deeply, we encourage you to reach out to them and learn more through their other channelled work, teaching, sessions or classes.

Most of all, we encourage you to take the time to absorb these words and from a place of heart-centeredness, shine your light that others may also find hope.

Breathe...be present...surrender... have faith, gratitude, and compassion... connect...take action...and most importantly...LOVE.

infinite strength
mind I body I soul

> **"Transform your life by integrating your mind, body, and soul."**

Counselling (Individual & Couples)
Hypnotherapy
Quantum Sound Therapy
Energy Healing (Reiki, IET, MDS, SRT)
Courses/Workshops
Personal Training (1-on-1 and 2-on-1)
Nutrition Coaching
& more

Anna Trillana & Andrew Bambury

🌐 www.infinitestrength.ca
✉ info@infinitestrength.ca
f infinitestrength.ca
◉ @infinitestrength.ca

Sparks of Healing

Do you live LIFE with Grace and Ease?

We can help you be the creator of your life experience!

Hypnosis

Soul Alignment

Reiki Sessions/Training

Spiritual Consultation

Sound Healing

(Remote options available)

Spark up your love of life!

- info@sparksofhealing.ca - www.sparksofhealing.ca -

Patricia Meier

Shooting Star Energies

Arianna Zimmer

Soul Alignment Practitioner

Transformational Leader

Spirited Guide and Coach

Coaching Packages

Private Channel &
Healing Sessions

Join me in the deep

exploration of what we are!

www.shootingstarenergies.com

Bonnie Bogner

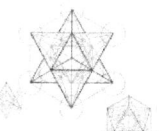

Galactic Council

Soul Vibrations
School of Light

We offer LIVE online training for

Soul Alignment Practitioner

Galactic Conversations
Channel Mentoring

Join our monthly
Galactic Council
Circle of Light

Personal Sessions
Soul Alignment & Channel

**Channel | Mystic | Coach | Intuitive | Author |
Spiritual Teacher | Retreat Facilitator**

Raising the vibration of the planet through LOVE...

**Website: bonniebogner.com
School: soul-vibrations.thinkific.com**

Made in the USA
Middletown, DE
27 December 2019